The Moscow Diaries:

Or, How I Stopped Worrying and Learned to Play the Post-Stalinist Blues

Richard Bryant

The Moscow Diaries

Copyright © 2007 by Richard Bryant

ISBN 978-0-61514-4999-8

www.themoscowdiaries.com

Acknowledgments

Thank you to my family and friends and everyone who helped make this journey possible. You know who you are.

Table of Contents

Introduction

This is the place to put the theories to the test. At least that's what I told myself when I arrived over one year ago. Theories ranging from cross-cultural sensitivity (as was drilled into my head in New York), methods of working in other languages, and ideas about living in Russia were dancing through my head like sugar plumbs on Christmas Eve. My theories are more sedate now, resting along the walls waiting to be asked to dance by some other theory or new idea. It didn't take me long to realize that I had to toss out most of what I thought I knew. That is except how to conjugate a Russian verb.

It usually begins like this. I am in some kind of gathering or meeting. I see that the group is at an impasse. It is an obstacle that churches in the United States have faced many times before. So I think, "Why reinvent the wheel?" I start to utter the words, "In the US, we've found that this works." So many times I have had to resist the urge to jump in and say, "This is how we do it so you should do it this way too." I'm very conscious about adding our institutional dysfunctions to their already present institutional dysfunctions. Then, I realize what I'm about to do, and I cut myself off mid sentence. I can't do that. What works at home won't necessarily work here. What works here won't work in the United States.

Usually these deadlocks revolve around logistic issues like property or the structure of committees in local organizations. I have realized how inadequate some of the structures developed for working in the United States are because they were not written with post-dictatorship countries in mind. It wasn't written for people who are only now coming to terms with the concept of private ownership of property. These simple issues can take hours and even days at a time to resolve. In one meeting shortly after I arrived, we discussed one sentence in a document for over an hour. It was the first sentence in the introductory paragraph. I turned to my colleague and said, "I now know why we won the Cold War." Remember, these are the Russians I am talking about. The Soviet Union perfected the art of inept and inefficient bureaucracy.

The questions about property, structure, and organization are important matters to be addressed. But these are not the most important challenges faced by the emerging church in the former USSR. Here's what I think the most important question is: Where do you start when you're starting from scratch? Where do you start when none of the normal rules apply? (Ok, I realize that's two questions.)

I find myself caught in the middle, living within the tension caused by unlearning one doctrine and embracing another.

It is impossible to fully grasp the effects of seventy years of Marxist-Leninist rule in this and the neighboring countries. The corrosive impact of Soviet policies toward the church as well as other elements of society has had a cumulative effect on the ethics, values, and morals of the entire population. At its heart, Russia is still a profoundly atheist nation, militantly atheist in some respects. Notwithstanding Vladimir Putin's regular television appearances where he is flanked by the Orthodox Patriarch or other Orthodox clergy, the Russian Orthodox Church remains on the periphery of society and removed from the daily lives of ordinary Russians. To witness the disconnect and the abandon with which most live, one need only observe the vast fortunes and extravagant lifestyles of the petroleum enriched elite.

It is a live fast, play hard, and die young world for many of those who have become wealthy in the past 15 years. At the other end of the spectrum you'll find the masses of people who live in a world where the average age of a Russian male is 56 years old. It seems difficult to believe that half of the people I see will not survive my first three years in Moscow. If I stay for a second tour, another 25 percent will die within that time. Lifestyle choices made by vast swathes of the Russian populous are killing the people faster than they can be replaced. That is a sign of great hopelessness and despair. That is the definition nihilism. That is the essence of atheism.

Hopelessness is not the sole preserve of the post-Communist atheists. Many believers, pastors and laypeople alike, are trying to maintain hope in the face of increasingly difficult odds.

Is that picture too dark? Maybe it is. It's also reality. Yet even within the darkness, hope remains. Where do I find hope? I find it in a theological concept that seems more appropriate in Russia than any other I've seen. It's called eschatology. It's a vast concept that may be new to some but even if you've never heard it before, you probably know what I mean. Eschatology is the study of the "end". I don't mean the "End" in the way the "Left Behind" books talk about the end. Some scholars and theologians argue that eschatology deals with interpreting and understanding Biblical prophecies that appear to foretell the end of time. I do not.

Eschatology is a way of living, to paraphrase Stephen Covey, with the "end" in mind. It's hard to live with the end in mind in the United

States. With the advances in medical science and technology (as well as our own obsessions with prolonging life at all cost) most of us don't live with the end in mind. We live as if we will live forever. Of course, there are notable exceptions. If you've faced a terminal illness or witnessed a loved one die too young and tragically, you probably have a different outlook. The vast majority of people do not live with that perspective. People who do are often characterized as morbid or diagnosed with depression or mental illness. For the most part, we live in a world that revolves around our own needs and desires. Even when we focus on others, we still focus on ourselves. Our families, our marriages, our jobs, our hobbies, our teams, it still comes back to "our" needs. We live focused on our next meeting, our next meal, our next vacation, or our next something.

When you know that you'll probably be dead well before you're 60, you live a little differently. You know you're not going to be here forever. If you're hopeless, you may live with total abandon and disregard for your health, life, or family. After all you're going to die soon anyway.

For a moment, consider first century Christianity. In the wake of Roman oppression and persecution, many Christian communities came to believe that the return of Christ was indeed imminent. The despair and hopelessness that surrounded them was palpable. In this environment, John of Patmos penned the Book of Revelation. He didn't want to scare people to death. He wanted to give them hope in the hopelessness. He too believed that time would soon come to a conclusion. In the midst of the "impending" demise, he wanted to paint a picture of reality beyond reality.

Sound familiar? I believe I am living in a place that is ripe for a message rooted in eschatological hope. It's a message that the Russians have heard many times before. In fact, an eschatological foundation is the key to understanding the Marxist message. Albeit a perversion of Christian eschatology, the skeletal framework was almost identical, borrowed from the German Lutherans who had been Marx's neighbors in early 19th century Germany. It was the theoretical basis underlying Communist teaching for 70 years. Instead of starting from an indefinable location called "the beginning"; I propose starting from "The End".

It is important to see where we are in Russia as part of a continuum of processes and thought. Some of what I write here may seem overly negative or pessimistic. It may be. However, I can say it is as honest a portrayal of what I'm seeing here.

Richard Bryant
Moscow, Russia
Summer 2007

Memoirs of a Moscow Weekend

I went to a birthday party on Saturday night. I know that's really nothing to write home about. It's not Earth shattering news to report that Richard Bryant attended a birthday party in Moscow. I realize this. If you write me to tell me this, ask yourself, what's the point of telling me something I already know? I did, however, wish to relate an anecdote from the evening's festivities.

The birthday "party" included a multi-cultural group of Georgians, Armenians, Russians, and at least one North Carolinian. (I was the North Carolinian). Throughout the course of the evening, conversations were flying around the table in at least four (sometimes five) different languages. I was the odd man out because I only spoke one other language well and could follow the Armenian to some degree. (Admittedly, I'm out of practice on the Armenian.) These people moved flawlessly between Russian, Armenian, Georgian, and English.

While they were gracious and incredibly welcoming, I couldn't help but feel I had missed the multi-lingual train. Coming from the country that has won more Nobel Prizes than any other in the world, a graduate of a pretty good university, and some linguistic facility, I still wasn't fluent in five languages. You've got to get out of the western hemisphere to realize how woefully lacking American education when it comes to languages. We only learn because something is practical. People are learning Spanish because it is practical and useful to their work. No one learns anything anymore for the sheer enjoyment of learning and appreciating the beauty of language. As the evening wore on, I felt like someone trying to learn how to play poker without ever being told the rules. That was until they changed the music.

Unlike most Russians I've met, these people have good taste in music. The radio stations here play a constant, if not nauseating stream of European techno or songs that passed their sell by date in America over twenty years ago. To be honest, I've been amazed at how broad a spectrum they've explored. Perhaps I should consider it a small miracle that I have met some people who feel the same way I do about Glenn Miller, Benny Goodman, Frank Sinatra, Louis Armstrong, Miles Davis, John Coltrane, Dean Martin, and most of the other luminaries of popular music who defined American jazz. One of their favorite pastimes is swing dancing in an open air Moscow park. They do this nearly every weekend. I can't tell you how liberating it is to have a conversation with someone who actually knows what I'm talking about!

One of the guests had brought a few CD's to listen to while we ate dinner. As we were eating, I noticed that the radio was playing a collection of familiar tunes that I hadn't heard in quite a while. I asked, "Is this the Squirrel Nut Zippers?"

"Yes," said the owner of the disc. "It is the Zippers. Have you heard of them?"

Have I heard of the Zippers? You bet I've heard of them. The Zippers are a retro swing band from the Chapel Hill/Carrboro area of central North Carolina. I first became aware of them as a sophomore in college. By the time I reached graduate school, they exploded onto the national music scene.

"I've seen them in concert," I said. "I know where they record their records."

A hush fell over the room.

"You have seen the Squirrel Nut Zippers. That is amazing," said one of the other guests. "Can you tell us, what is a Squirrel Nut Zipper, what does this mean?"

"It's a candy bar that became popular in the United States in the 1920's."

There were nods of approval and understanding going around the entire table. It was as if they couldn't believe that sitting here in their midst was a real American who had seen their favorite band. They knew the music, the lyrics in English (though they usually didn't understand what they were saying), and even the names of the band members. For much of the rest of the evening, they peppered me with questions that I did my best to answer.

Do you know how long it's been since I've been the coolest guy in the room because of my esoteric musical knowledge?

About as long as it's been since I went swing dancing with people who know what they're doing.

About as long as it's been since I voluntarily went watch a play in Georgian.

Memo from the Home Office in Moscow, Russia

You can imagine there were many tense and uncomfortable moments during the return trip to Moscow. I guess his curiosity was understandable. For years, this man absorbed the Orthodox line about Protestants and Americans and their evil machinations to destroy Russian society. Now, as if by some divine miracle, he had a real live honest to God in the flesh Protestant as his virtual prisoner for the next eleven or so hours. This was clearly an opportunity that he didn't want to pass up.

I know the image many people have of Christian do-gooders in general is of people who are always willing and excited to talk with strangers. While this may come as a shock to some, there are times when I am not excited, willing, or even anxious to discuss theology. I'll admit it, I was exhausted and in no mood to do any of this. I wanted to be left alone. I hadn't bathed in over four days. I smelled so bad that I could barely stand to be in my own presence. I looked even worse. Blood shot eyes, mosquito bites on every extremity, unshaven, and unclean; the farthest thing from my mind was engaging a militant Orthodox nationalist in some kind of debate that was impossible to win.

No matter what I said or how well I said it, he wasn't going to be convinced. In a way, I didn't want to convert him to or from anything. He was obviously a Christian. His beliefs were as deeply held and as important to him as mine are to me. Who am I to tell him he's wrong? Remember, he had no problem pointing out how wrong I was to even be in Russia and ask why I couldn't just go home.

The antipathy many ultra-Orthodox Russians hold towards Protestants is hard to describe for Americans. As one who doesn't like to be deterred by the confines of language, I'll give it a try. Lawyers, Madonna fans, drug addicts, and Communists are held in higher regard than American protestant missionaries. He made that quite clear.

Remember the old dictum about never discussing religion and politics? If you do what I do, it is never possible to avoid religion or politics. It is even harder when the people around you don't share the same sense of conversational decorum. As one of the few Americans many Russians have met or may ever meet, I become the logical beneficiary of their many criticisms of everything that is wrong about American culture and foreign policy. They may never get to talk to George W. Bush, so Richard L. Bryant will have to do. I'm not certain if they expect me to forward their comments along to the White House or the God worshipped by Protestants (their phrase, not mine). When you're trapped in a tiny room on a train, there is really no place to hide. You're stuck. You're trapped.

"What does your family think about what you do?" he asked.

"They are supportive," I replied.

"They are not ashamed?"

"Nope," I said, hoping the one word answers would begin to slow him down.

He was clearly flummoxed. How could any self-respecting American family allow their only son to go to Russia to convert people who didn't need to be converted in the first place? I realized that he wanted me to comment on his apparent disbelief so before he could regroup and continue his denunciation of my career and family, I decided to try and end the conversation or at least start throwing out verbal speed bumps. Since he had moved toward the subject of families, I thought this might be a good way out.

"You said you had a family?" I asked. I remembered he had mentioned something two hours earlier about daughters. Families are safe subjects, right?

"Yes, I have two daughters. One is thirteen and the other is ten."

"What wonderful ages!" "Teenagers can be such joy," I exclaimed.

"Net, it is a very difficult age," he replied. I could tell that he was pleased that I asked about his family but his face bore that same fatigued expression of parents all over the world.

Now that I had reestablished some of my humanity by asking about his family, I moved to the second step in my grand strategy to kill the conversation.

"Did you have brothers and sisters when you were growing up here in Voronezh?"

"Yes, I had a brother and a sister." He didn't seem that eager to talk about his family. So I decided to dig a little deeper.

"Which one of you did your parents love more?"

"What do you mean?" he asked in Russian.

"I mean which one of you did your parents love more."

He gave no answer. Maybe he was waiting for a response from me. I think he believed that this was some kind of clever rhetorical device to illustrate how God is the same, regardless of language or culture, and loves everyone equally. It wasn't that. This was my reward for having to listen to his diatribes. If he was determined to make me uncomfortable, the least I could do was to return the favor.

With every passing moment, my questions became gradually more, well, weird. After a few more queries about the average rainfall in the Voronezh area and the popularity of pigs as household pets in the Caucasus, we had moved far away from religion enough for him to decide that sleep was a much preferable option than a continued, albeit one sided, "dialogue".

Just before he turned in for the night, he did manage to sneak one more question under the wire. "What would you think if Russians came to America and tried to convert Methodists or Protestants?"

"That would be fine," I said. "We would have no problem with that."

Maybe that's not entirely accurate. I know educated people in the research triangle area of North Carolina who still believe that Catholics aren't really Christian. I can just see Russian priests in long black cassocks going door to door in subdivisions where the median home price is $750,000. How long would it take before someone called the sheriff's department? Probably not long at all.

Fear and Loathing on the Train to Moscow

"Watch out for the snakes."

-Remark of a Speedo wearing fat man who was fishing by the river where I was preparing to swim on Saturday afternoon.

If you believe what you hear on Sunday mornings, witnessing is supposed to be easy. Ok, maybe not easy. Yet the glossy versions told on Sunday mornings, in DVD series, and in hundreds of books make it sound that way. The theory is that when people discover what you do or if they see you reading a Bible or religious text, they will be intrigued and want to talk with you about your faith. If I have heard one "success" story I've heard a hundred. After a conversation on a plane or train with a Christian, these people are miraculously led to a relationship with Jesus Christ-sometimes even before landing or arrival. While I don't doubt the veracity of their testimonies, these stories do not bear any resemblance to the reality I have experienced in Russia. Take last night for example.

I'm on the train back to Moscow. There are also three Russian men who are sharing the compartment. One of the three speaks a little English. He had been in the Soviet Merchant Navy and had visited the United States on many occasions. After the normal exchange of pleasantries and greetings in two languages, we settled into a comfortable silence. I was reading a book by the French philosopher Bernard-Henri Levy. On my Ipod, I was listening to Sam Cooke's live performance from the Harlem Square Club in 1963. Not a bad way to chill out after a particularly demanding annual conference.

After a while, I got up to go to the bathroom. When I returned, my new friend asked me about my life, my family, and my job. I told him I worked for the United Methodist Church. It was clear that he didn't quite grasp what I was saying. He seemed to think I worked for a pro-democracy western NGO designed to undermine the authority of the Russian government. It took about fifteen more minutes and a much longer explanation in Russian before he finally understood. Almost immediately, I could see his countenance change and the entire conversation shifted.

"I do not like what you are doing," he said. He went on to explain many of the traditional Orthodox arguments against the presence of foreign missionaries (or non-Orthodox religious groups) working in Russia. Many devout Russian Orthodox believers view Orthodoxy as synonymous with Russian national identity. If you are Russian, born in Russia of Russian parents, then you are Orthodox. There are no alternatives. Russia is Christian and Orthodox. In this world view, they see no need or reason for any other Christian groups to be in Russia.

I tried to explain to him that the freedom to worship also included a freedom to choose where one worships. I asked, "Do people not have the right to choose where they go to church?" His answer was clear. No, they do not. Russian means Orthodox and Orthodox means Russian. There was no room to maneuver.

Of course, we believe they do have this right and should be allowed to exercise it. The Orthodox, however, do not share this opinion. Aggressive proselytizing is viewed as a threat to the Russian national identity and security. When your religious identity and national identity are synonymous, a perceived threat to religious security is treated like any other national security concern. To the devout Orthodox nationalists, our presence is making Russia less safe and less secure. This man told me that he believes protestant missionaries are, "undermining the social fabric of an already fragile Russian society." That's why, even though the Methodist Church is registered and technically "legal" in Russia, we still have to be careful. As I've seen, the law affords protection to those who assassinate journalists and political dissidents. If assassins aren't prosecuted, who's going to stop anyone from going after an unwanted protestant missionary or church?

We talked well into the night. I learned a long time ago that one can't win an argument with an ideologue. For that reason, I detest ideologues-people who are so convinced of the rightness and moral superiority of their own positions they are unable to acknowledge the possibility that alternatives might exist. My goal was to articulate my position as clearly and as lovingly as possible. If anything, I hoped what I said sounded reasonable, rational, and sane. I even conceded that he had valid points. I can truly understand how the Orthodox feel and why they want to lay a special claim on the souls of ordinary Russians. I understand the position, though I don't agree with it.

In most classes and seminars I've seen on witnessing, people talk about discussing the four spiritual laws and the need to stress the importance of having Jesus as your "friend" and "savior" (even though the later concept is completely foreign to most of the unchurched we need to reach). Jesus of Nazareth is presented in simplistic terms as someone to help you with your problems-sort of a spiritual coping mechanism. None have included topics such as "How to discuss complex issues of freedom and choice in a post modern, post-totalitarian society in a language other than your native tongue." Luckily, I had done some independent study. Thank God for that.

What's my point? At 9:30 in the morning and after only one cup of coffee, I'm not too sure. I believe it is simply this: it's not as easy as it looks. It's not as easy to talk about your faith as many religious professionals make it sound. It takes more knowledge than can be found in seminars, testimonies, and books sold only at Christian bookstores. To engage the world we must be prepared to move and exist beyond the comfortable confines of the Christian bubbles that we call home.

His last words to me were, "I can't wish you luck in your job and what you do." I thanked him for his kindness and wished him well. That's a great way to start a Monday morning at 8:00 am after having slept less than three hours on an overnight train from Voronezh. That's Russia. That's reality. That's living in Russia in the 21st century. As Dean Martin once said, "Ain't that a kick in the head."

The Last Tango in Voronezh
When the Going Gets Weird the Weird Go to Annual Conference

In which the links of coincidence are forged into the chain of fate.

Albert Camus once wrote that the loves we share with cities are often secret loves. Though I complain bitterly and often about Russia's cities, I am secretly in love with each of these disparate places. Moscow is a city that is all things to all people at once. St. Petersburg is the elegant exemplar of all things cultural and a constant reminder of Russia's more glorious past. Yekaterinburg is like the younger sister of St. Petersburg and Moscow, forever vying for attention amid her more glamorous siblings. They are each like exotic foreign mistresses, enticing and alluring in their own ways and distinctive charms. Observations like this are easy to make when you're sitting in a Moscow café, sipping Turkish coffee and enjoying the beautiful weather. They are much harder to make when you're actually there.

Conference accommodations are a role of the dice when it comes to Russia. Like Forrest's box of chocolates, you never know what you're going to get. I knew I was in trouble when I saw the name of the hotel. If you have to put the word "class" or "classy" in your name, it is a good indication that the place you are running will have neither class nor taste, that is, unless your definitions of class and taste include decaying socialist architecture. The nicest possible thing to say is that it is an action of overcompensation. Ok, maybe that's not fair. The place was only $12.00 a night. One can't expect too much from a hotel that offers that kind of a bargain. I would soon discover that for the same 12 dollars a night, one can't expect seats on the toilet, toilet paper or the absence of mice in your room. That was last week's hotel in Yekaterinburg. The place reminded me of Belgrade in the mid 1990's. If I ever needed a cheap place to shoot a Yugoslavian war epic-I now know where I would go.

Voronezh is another matter altogether. The accommodations, set among the picturesque pines of the southern steppe, bear a striking resemblance to Colonel Kurtz's compound at the end of Apocalypse Now. Once you arrive at the camp, you do feel as if you've arrived, at "The End". I have trouble categorizing my relationship with Voronezh. It is a city of one million people in the industrial heartland of southern Russia. It is a hard place to love, though in the old town, there are some beautiful tree lined streets that do exude an old world charm. There are some long hard miles between Moscow and Voronezh. For most people (missionaries, conscripts, and tea smugglers), they begin in the early evening haze of cigarette smoke and body odor that is Paveletskaya Station. There aren't many amenities for the business traveler or casual tourists at Paveletskaya. Though if your needs run toward cheap beer or greasy Central Asian lamb, you'll never be disappointed.

Like most Russian train stations, Paveletskaya Station on a Thursday night in May is where Moscow ends and the frontier begins. It is a place where one can already feel the rules and order of society beginning to change. In every group of two or three people, I was constantly waiting for a fight to break out or someone to be thrown across the sidewalk. Think about the bar scene from the first Star Wars movie but with fewer reptile like aliens, more Slavic techno-pop, and the same shady smugglers looking to escape the Empire's storm troopers.

The storm troopers were everywhere. Hundreds of Russian soldiers seem to be always heading south. I guess they have to go where the action is. From garrison towns like Voronezh and places all down this same rail line, Russian troops have traveled to fight Chechens and other Caucasian tribes for the better part of two hundred years.

The 8:50 to Voronezh is not a historic train in the same way as the Red Arrow. The Red Arrow has a seventy-five year history of taking travelers in style from Moscow to St. Petersburg. The Voronezh train is short on style but long on number of cars. It is a friendly train, with the exception of the staff, especially for people traveling alone. Most Russians are far friendlier on trains than on the buses or the metro. Maybe, because they know they will be sharing a cramped space for over eight hours, the walls of their normally icy Slavic reserve begin to crumble.

It is not unheard of for passengers to bring along their dinner on such early evening train journeys. These are literally picnics on rails. (Russian trains aren't known for the quality of their dining cars.) If they do follow such a custom, they will usually bring enough to share with their traveling companions. As I hadn't eaten, I was hoping I would be on the receiving end of some Slavic hospitality. One of the three sharing the car had brought an assortment of breads, boiled potatoes and chicken. Admittedly, it wasn't a bad buffet.

While I enjoyed their hospitality and my inclusion in their conviviality, I should have known better of eating food from unknown Russians. By 1:30 am, when I was suffocating from the lack of ventilation and air in the compartment, my stomach was in the throws of a full scale revolution. I believe it was the chicken. I will never know for sure. I do know that I spent the better part of the next three hours sitting in the tiny cabinet that passed for the train's toilet. The rest of the night I tossed and turned like an epileptic heroin addict making the transition to methadone. It didn't end there. I was in and out of the bathroom all day. This is what I get for trying to be friendly and engaging!

As the previous week, I was carrying nearly two dozen copies of the Book of Discipline. My bags looked more like I had just robbed a Circuit City and a Cokesbury store by trying to stuff everything into in a small rolling suitcase. In addition to the books, I had one laptop computer, two cell phones, one PDA, a half a dozen cables, two power supplies, one Ipod, a quart of Soviet army issue Mosquito repellant, one bottle of Texas Pete, one bottle of Tabasco sauce, Tylenol, Ibuprofen, Imodium, and enough Wellbutrin to keep me sane until sometime Monday morning.

By 8:00 am, I was dehydrated, dazed, and pulling into the train station. I was back in Voronezh. As Waylon Jennings once said, "the First time the devil made me do it but the second time I came back on my own."

The Book of Discipline

Domededovo Airport

"Book of Discipline?" the guard asked. The security guard wasn't sure if he had only misunderstood my Russian or had indeed heard me correctly.

"Yes," I said. "I'm taking these books (I left out the "of Discipline") to a meeting in Yekaterinburg." I was careful to pronounce the "u" in the same way the French pronounce the port of Cherbourg. I didn't want to sound like any Johnny come lately foreigner. Russians cringe when Americans (or any foreigner for that matter) pronounce the names of any of their cities that end in "burg" by saying "berg". It's a dead give away that you're not from around these Siberian parts.

By the time I approached the security point, I had already checked in for the overcrowded flight to Yekaterinburg. There are really few words in the English language to describe the experience of checking in for a Russian flight. Like most other places of waiting for means of transportation in Russia, the most important point to remember is when you arrived in the line and when your turn should come has no bearing whatsoever on when you might actually get to the front of the line or be seen by an agent. That is if there is an agent at all. Russian airport check-in lines are not places for claustrophobics or those who have issues with personal space. You can perform prostate surgery with a lesser degree of intimacy than is needed to check-in to a budget Russian airline.

This morning, I was in possession of forty large, hardback books that were clearly titled in a large bold Cyrillic font as "The Book of Discipline." This guard had never searched an American carrying a case of books marked in such a strange way. It was even clearer he didn't know what to do with me. Had this been fifteen years earlier, I would have been looking at serious jail time. Thankfully, those times have changed. Perhaps he was wishing he had picked someone else for his random search. Regardless of his initial motivations, because of the bulky contents of my high end Russian luggage (i.e. a cardboard box wrapped in blue cellophane) he was now suspicious and wasn't about to let me pass without further and more careful inspection. For all he knew, these imposing volumes were a set of the complete works of the Marquis de Sade that I would be using to lead a seminar on new bondage techniques for the sexually repressed people of western Siberia.

"What are the books about?" he finally got around to asking.

"About?"

He wanted to know this book I was carrying was all about?. Was he trying to trick me? Was this some kind of interrogation technique? That's a question many pastors couldn't answer on the floor of an annual conference. I was being asked by an armed Russian airport security guard. If a pastor or "religious professional" couldn't give an answer, she or he might get moved the following year or be denigrated at cover dish suppers by parishioners when they are sure the pastor is out of ear shot. If I gave a wrong answer or my ego began writing checks that my body couldn't cash, what was to stop him from shooting me? I've been in some pretty contentious church committee meetings but none ever ended in an execution behind the fellowship hall-at least as far as I know.

The last time I was asked about the meaning of the Book of Discipline no one dared to ask such a simple question. Nor did anyone on the Board of Ordained Ministry ask me how I would define the purpose and role of the Discipline to a coterie of skeptical Russian airline security guards. Evidently, I thought, the guard was starting with the tough interrogation questions. My first response was to say that it isn't really about anything. I defy the most adept of Wesley scholars to find any unifying theme linking the Discipline's many disparate paragraphs. The Metho-Nerds would probably answer, "Connectionalism". The irony is that most of the people who would give such an answer wouldn't know real connectionalism if it side swiped them at rush hour on the interstate.

"It is about the Methodist Church," I finally said.

"The protestant sect?" he replied.

If I hadn't been trying to catch a flight (or been confronting a man with an automatic weapon), this might have been an ideal opportunity to witness about my faith. For a moment, I even thought about giving him a copy of the book. However, I didn't have that luxury and decided that as a witnessing tool the Book of Discipline would do more harm than good. There are parts of the Book of Discipline that make the IRS Tax Code read like Shakespearean sonnets.

"Yes, the book is about how the church should operate. It is something like canon law in the Orthodox Church-a rule book."

"Why not call it Canon Law?"

I guess that would either make too much sense or sound too traditional. Yet, honestly, how "with it" does the "Book of Discipline" sound?

It doesn't. However, if it could function as a conversation starter, maybe we need to be more visible about our Discipline and try to figure out what it really means. All of this and I hadn't even left Moscow.

May Day, May 9th (or How to Offend a Russian's Sensibilities)

May 9th may be the most important national holiday in the Russian Federation. To make a comparison with the United States, it is a day which combines the elements and emotions of Veterans Day, Memorial Day, and the Fourth of July. Unlike most Americans who regard the aforementioned days as breaks and vacations, not quasi-religious festivals to remember the sacrifices of war dead, most Russians take these days seriously. I know this because I am here. While I recognize the sacred significance of May 9th in the Russian calendar of secular holy days, it was hard not to laugh at the spectacle of thousands of Communists marching through the center of Moscow. Fifteen years after the official demise of the USSR, both the old and young gathered to watch aged Soviet veterans parade under red banners proclaiming "All Power to the Soviets". The parade I witnessed wasn't the military spectacle unfolding a block away in Red Square. This parade was truly more about the "war". This second parade, under the guise of honoring the genuine sacrifice of the millions of ordinary Soviets citizens and soldiers in World War II, was a chance to pretend that the Soviet Union is still something it never really was, great.

Despite the comedic spectacle of thousands of people honoring one of the greatest political failures of modern time, it was, perhaps more appalling to see Russian pensioners proudly holding portraits of Joseph Stalin. It is illegal to hold a parade in the Federal Republic of Germany while carrying pictures of Adolph Hitler. You can be locked up for denying the holocaust, in Austria, even if the denial occurred in a language other than German and in a different country. Just ask David Irving, a British scholar and holocaust denier who sits in a Vienna prison. (I will not address the many anti-Semitic signs and posters carried by the marchers. These were equally disgusting and were clearly displayed amid the varied Soviet symbols. While the poverty of the Russian pensioners is deplorable, anti-Semitism is inexcusable regardless of your socio-economic status.)

In Russia, it is not a crime to honor Stalin's wretched memory. In fact, it is encouraged. Mussolini's memory remains banned in Italy. Hitler's likeness is banned from all public German discourse. Only Stalin remains a palpable figure in his native land. Why? This isn't a time to debate the merits of unfettered free speech. It is though a chance to ask why the Russians have trouble acknowledging the facts about one of the twentieth century's most horrific figures. What is it about the Italians and Germans that is lacking in the Russians? Perhaps it is a Slavic "thing". The Bosnian Serbs refuse to handover Ratko Mladic and Radovan Karadzic to this day. These two men have the blood of thousands of Bosnians on their hands but remain both free and national heroes to Serbs and Slavs everywhere.

That, in and of itself, speaks volumes about how the past is re-membered in modern Russia. Despite the bloody purges, the man made famines, thousands of executions carried out on his direct orders, and the strategic stupidity of the Molotov-Ribbentrop Pact that virtually guaranteed Germany's near defeat of the Soviet Union, Stalin remains the stern, yet admirable father figure. On many occasions, I've heard Russians too young to have any firsthand knowledge of Stalin's brutality say, "We Russians need someone like Stalin to keep us in line. We can't cope with democ-racy." What is so surprising about this language is that it comes from the Russians themselves, people who should know the full extent of Stalin's brutality. One expected to hear such things from fellow travelers like Jean-Paul Sartre in the 1950's, not from Russians in the year 2007. If ordinary Russians feel that way about a man who died in 1953, is it any wonder that Vladimir Putin has the support of the vast majority of the Russian public? No.

Vladimir Lenin's body still lies on Red Square and Joseph Stalin's picture is still carried throughout the streets. If the Soviet Union is really dead, why not let it all go? This is because ideology and national identity remain synonymous in Russia. It is impossible to separate one from the other. Russia may no longer be the Soviet superpower but the ideology which guided their course through seventy years remains as firmly entrenched as ever. When I say ideology, I am not referring to an adherence to Marxist-Leninist doctrine. This is the ideological identity of being history's perpetual victims. Russia remains the red-headed stepchild of the grand European experiment and because of its unique geography and history of conquest from outside invaders, became determined to be the bully and never be conquered again.

The Russians remain touchy about criticizing Stalin or really any elements of their Soviet past. A fitting parallel can be found in Martin Scorsese's 1990 gangster epic, "GoodFellas". In one scene, Tommy DeVito (played by Joe Pesci), plays an on edge Mafioso extremely sensitive to any disrespect or personal attacks. His companion, Henry Hill (played by Ray Liotta), often takes the brunt of his anger, as this snippet of dialogue shows:

Henry Hill: You're a pistol, you're really funny. You're really funny.
Tommy DeVito: What do you mean I'm funny?

Henry Hill: It's funny, you know. It's a good story, it's funny, you're a funny guy.

[laughs]

Tommy DeVito: what do you mean, you mean the way I talk? What?

Henry Hill: It's just, you know. You're just funny, it's… funny, the way you tell the story and everything.

Tommy DeVito: [it becomes quiet] Funny how? What's funny about it?

Anthony Stabile: Tommy no, You got it all wrong.

Tommy DeVito: Oh, oh, Anthony. He's a big boy, he knows what he said. What did ya say? Funny how?

Henry Hill: Jus…

Tommy DeVito: What?

Henry Hill: Just… ya know… you're funny.

This is most clearly seen in Russia's ongoing diplomatic spat with Estonia regarding latter's decision to move a Soviet war memorial from downtown Tallinn to a military cemetery outside of town. It would be funny if this same dialogue had not been played out by the Russians, Estonians, and the European Union on CNN. It is clear that countries (be they former Soviet republics or the United States of America) can say what they want to say or do what they want to do as long as it doesn't offend the ever moving bar of what is offensive to those calling the shots in contemporary Russia. The Russians have been more upset about moving the war memorial in Estonia than US missile systems being placed in Poland or the Czech Republic.

The slightest of perceived insults will bring the verbal, economic, and electronic wrath of the entire Russian political apparatus. The disproportionate anger can be as entertaining as it is sinister. Watching the foreign minister become apoplectic with rage, one would think the west had just launched a unilateral nuclear strike on Russia's major cities. Like Prague in 1968 or Budapest in 1956, it is not hard to believe that if they could get away with it, the Russians would have reoccupied Estonia by force to ensure that the monument was not moved. Instead of invading tanks, rail links are severed because of track and safety concerns. Gas lines are cut because of questions about the stability of the pipeline. The Estonian embassy is placed under a virtual state of siege by pro-Kremlin youth. All pretenses of diplomatic protection are suspended for the Estonians and other embassies conducting business with the Estonians. These actions are designed to send a clear and unmistakable message: don't think about questioning us. If you do question, we will use whatever means at our disposal to hurt you. If that means economic measures, so be it. If it means assassination, then so be it. What does the world do? We watch passively and pretend that Russia is on the path to democracy and that the Soviet ideology is an outdated historical anachronism in the modern Russian state. We delude ourselves. We tell ourselves lies because it is simply too hard to believe and act otherwise.

As their logic goes, because the Soviets bore the heavy losses from the German army on the eastern front and helped rid the world of "fascism", one cannot criticize the brutal totalitarian system that predated the war, existed during the war, postdated the war, and killed twice as many of its own people as the Germans killed in all of the concentration camps combined. Could the allies have defeated Nazi Germany without the contributions of the Soviet Army? Yes. It would have taken far longer and cost more lives but it would have eventually happened. If nothing else, President Truman had an option that the Soviet Union had yet to steal, the Atomic Bomb.

In an essay entitled, "How to Write about Lenin-and How Not To", the Roman Catholic moral philosopher Alastair MacIntyre wrote that the greatest (or unpardonable) sin of the historian is to be patronizing. In other words, if you cannot imagine or do not attempt to place yourself in the historical context of a given situation then you should keep your historical assessments to yourself. MacIntyre's point is if you want to understand Lenin, one needs to try to understand the background events of 1905 and the days leading up to the October Revolution of 1917. He's correct. I can see why many Russians might long for the simpler time and stability of the not so distant Soviet past. Yet, for the countless numbers of people carrying Stalin's portrait on a sunny Wednesday afternoon, I am afraid that they have either forgotten or do not care to imagine the conditions in places like the Siberian slave labor camps or the basement cells of Lubyanka Prison. If that is truly the case, then this is as good as things will ever be in this place called Russia.

To paraphrase Voltaire, to the living we owe respect. To the dead, we owe the truth.

Slavic Body Odor

If you heard my interview on NPR, I expressed a newfound respect and admiration for the Russian people. After waiting for an hour and forty-five minutes to view the body of Boris Yeltsin, I saw a different side to the Russian psyche that wasn't as gruff and aggressive as I have often portrayed. It was a moving and humbling experience. However, for all of the good feeling and emotion, I am still having trouble coming to grips with the pervasive Slavic body odor. My time outside the Christ the Savior Cathedral may have helped me to better understand the Russian argot of shoving and pushing that defines each bus ride, metro trip, or McDonald's order. Yet it did nothing to increase my patience or graciousness when it comes to living with some of the foulest odors known to man.

It is hard to ignore the smells of unwashed bodies and unclean clothes. After more than a year behind the still rusting Iron Curtain, I am unable to rationalize, emotionalize, or otherwise come to terms with the daily onslaught of gag reflex inducing odors. These are odors coming from the people who are still wrestling with western notions of personal space. On that very evening, no sooner than I descended the metro stairs toward the subway train, I was hit once again with the familiar fragrance of hundreds of unwashed Slavs crammed onto subway trains. As the weather warms it will only get worse. I honestly believe that there are some people who haven't washed their clothes or themselves all winter long.

Russia may be the world's smelliest country. The awesome prepotency of this ongoing olfactory assault is no mere sensory illusion. There are few places on Earth where one can find the potent mix of coal smoke, diesel fumes, industrial effluvia, homemade alcohol, and body odor seamlessly woven (or should I say embedded) into the fabric of daily life. It's not that cleanliness is a cost-prohibitive financial decision on par with the purchase of an armor plated Land Rover. Soaps, detergents, and dry cleaners are widely available throughout the city.

Most Russian dry cleaners charge a fraction of what their counterparts in the United States demand to clean ties, suits, and dresses. Even by those standards and the general worldwide decline in the value of the dollar, the ability to have one's clothes cleaned is well within the range of the most meager salaries and pensions. If money isn't an obstacle to clean clothes and running water isn't a scarce commodity, what other plausible explanation exists for the never ending cycle of nausea caused by the unwashed masses? There isn't one. There is no explanation other than the deliberate choices made by thousands of Russians not to wash clothes or bathe their bodies. The decision to be dirty is a choice and a lifestyle decision, not the embodiment of an age old cultural practice.

Is there anything that the Russians can't stand to smell? I began to ask this question shortly after my arrival. I didn't really come up with an answer until sometime last autumn. It was late one evening and I was traveling by train from Moscow to the industrial city of Voronezh. If anywhere could smell worse than Moscow, it is Voronezh. But I wasn't in Voronezh. I was sitting in a four person train compartment with three other Russians, one of whom fell firmly into the nauseatingly smelly category. We hadn't left Moscow. Two minutes after making my way onto the train, I was well on my way to full scale civil war between my nose and my gastrointestinal tract.

My first instinct was to "out smell the smeller" by some other means. I knew this to be the most theologically appropriate thing I could do. After all, had not St. Augustine in The City of God, said as much? I know that the Bishop of Hippo is not known for his levity, yet he does make mention of men who "have such command of their bowels, that they can break wind continuously at will, so as to produce the effect of singing." Yes, says Augustine, before the fall of Adam and Eve in the Garden of Eden, humanity sang praises to God through flatulence. Can you imagine how that would alter the American religious landscape today? Can you imagine the interviews for worship leaders? Augustine attributes the loss of this skill to the original sin of Adam and Eve and it consequences with respect to body control.

Using this radical Augustinian approach, I could find the dining car and load up on as much Diet Coke, beans, lentils, milk, onions, radishes, sweet potatoes, cheese, cashews, Jerusalem artichokes, oats, and other vegetables. The big drawback with this idea was I would not only be subjecting the smeller to my odors but two innocent people as well. The combination of his body odor and my own internal odors was not a viable alternative, now matter how theologically sound.

When the train finally did pull out of the station, I decided to go for a walk. Even if I had to spend the night in this gas chamber on rails; I could at least postpone the inevitable for a few more minutes. Not that there are lots of places to go walking on a Russian train. Walking in search of fresh air on a Russian train isn't something that one does easily or quickly. First, you must make your way past countless others who are watching the countryside roll by in the darkness. At the end of the car, you will reach a heavy door that leads to a rickety metal vestibule connecting the two cars. Invariably, these are the areas where the smokers congregate. From past experience, I knew that someone will be smoking in these areas throughout the night, forming a second line of defense against would be terrorists and thieves. The common area linking the two cars was crowded with smokers and despite the wind blowing through cracks in the floor and the accordion like material linking the train's sections, the stink was still there. It was then I remembered my own "ace in the hole".

I had, stored somewhere within my luggage, a Cohiba Churchill. For those of you who do not know what I am talking about, a Cohiba is a brand of cigar-a product of Fidel Castro's oppressive Cuban regime and is named after a former British Prime Minister who enjoyed their particular flavor. I wondered what would happen if I, in this impromptu smoking lounge, decided to smoke the Cohiba. Unlike many American bars and restaurants (or at least those that still allow smoking) there were no signs prohibiting the consumption of tobacco through pipes or cigars.

Quickly, I made my way back to the sleeping compartment and found the cigar, still snug in its distinctive case. Within moments, I returned to the rolling smokers' convention. Careful not to give the game up too soon, I lit the cigar in the hall just prior to stepping out into the night air. It didn't take long before the Russians were holding their own noses and making their way back to their own compartments. I had finally found something that the Russians couldn't stand to smell. Thank you, Mr. Castro.

Boris Yeltsin (1931-2007)

In 1931, the year Boris Yeltsin was born; Joseph Stalin ordered the dynamiting of Moscow's largest Russian Orthodox Cathedral, "Christ the Savior." Last night, along with thousands of other ordinary Muscovites, I waited to file past Yeltsin's casket in Christ the Savior Cathedral, a church that Yeltsin ordered to be rebuilt. History has come full circle. Even in death Boris Yeltsin is still making history. Beginning around 2pm this afternoon, the centuries old Orthodox funeral liturgy, led by the Patriarch of All Russia, will be held for the first leader of post-Soviet Russia.

Instead of the dour images of Soviet funerals where the Communist Party buried leaders like Brezhnev, Andropov, and Chernenko, the Russian Orthodox Church and the Russian people are burying a retired pensioner and politician albeit an extremely influential retiree. Instead of a granite statue by the Kremlin wall, this man will be buried in Moscow's most historic and religiously significant cemetery, adjacent to a medieval Russian monastic fortress. This will be the first time the Russian Orthodox Church has officiated at the funeral of a Russian head of state since Czar Alexander III died in 1894. What the world is seeing in Russia today is no small historical moment.

It might be argued that this alcoholic politician, who began life as provincial Soviet functionary, did more to revitalize religious life in post-Soviet Russia than any other figure. He wasn't known to be a particularly pious or religious man. But Boris Yeltsin recognized the role that traditional Orthodox Christianity played in the lives of ordinary Russians. In a time of great societal and economic changes, I believe that he and his advisors realized that a renewed church and a revitalized faith were important if Russia was to survive the initial pains of the transition from a planned economy to free-market capitalism. It was Boris Yeltsin who ordered the removal of Lenin's museum from inside the Kremlin walls. Yeltsin also ordered the destruction of the "House of Special Purposes." This was the building in Yekaterinburg (Yeltsin's hometown) where Czar Nicholas II and the Russian royal family were executed in the summer of 1918. On the site where the house once stood, is a massive Russian Orthodox cathedral, dedicated to the memory of the Romanov martyrs.

The crowds waiting to see Russia's first president were a cross-section of the entire city. Young people, old people, rich people, poor people; they all came to pay their final respects to Yeltsin. Most were carrying single roses to lay by the side of his flag-draped casket. Others were visibly shaking, crying, and overwhelmed with emotion. It was amazing for me, as someone who has developed a somewhat cynical view of the Russian people, to witness this vast outpouring of grief and emotion. People were genuinely moved and wanted to express their sense of loss in a variety of personal ways. Unlike most of my other experiences waiting in Russian lines, this one was orderly, peaceful, and quiet. There was no pushing and shoving. I only saw a few people speaking on their cell phones. In Moscow, Russians are always talking to other Russians on their cell phones. Not last night. I made a couple of quick phone calls but it was clear that this wasn't a typical line on a typical Russian Tuesday night.

As I walked out of the cathedral doors toward the phalanx of the world's news media, a Russian television reporter from one of their major networks stepped in front of me.

"Don't you want to talk to a Russian?" I said.

"No, I'd like to talk to someone different," he replied.

"Can you do an interview in Russian?"

I said I could try. That's what we did. From the outset, I wasn't certain of how well I did. In fact, I was absolutely certain I looked like a complete idiot.

So if you were watching Russian television in late April and saw an extremely nervous American trying to speak his best grammatically correct Russian, it was me.

It's Not about God

The "we just wanna" prayers will be coming thick and fast over the next few days in churches all across America. Those familiar words of diminutive servitude will ring forth as people of faith try to put the tragic events on Virginia Tech's campus into some kind of religious perspective. Because we (those who lead American churches) have created a culture of people who begin their prayers as if prayer is so much of an inconvenience to God that we must preface our most intimate thoughts with the oh so contemporary, "we just" (...I hate to get in your way God, but we just want...), as if God could care less about God's most precious creations and is busier with more onerous responsibilities, the groundwork has already been laid to explain how God could "allow" such evil to occur.

"We just wanna say that everything happens in your divine plan..."

I'm going to try and head off some of the religious garbage that will come following the coverage of the tragedy in Blacksburg. As the week goes on, I know that some of my more fundamentalist brothers and sisters will try and explain the events of Monday morning in terms of "God's will". It is the nature of our modern world. It happens after most major crises and tragedies. Because some Christians lack the theological depth to explain the most fundamental questions about humanity, evil, and God's relationship to the two, they find it easier to say, "It was God's will" or "it was just their time".

For the record, let me state, the God I believe in does not sanction evil, murder, violence, disease, death, pestilence, or genocide. Evil defies rationality or explanation. To believe that it is God's will that people are murdered or are appointed to die at a particular time and place is not only stupid (the equivalent of theological child abuse) but it is a perversion of the most basic premises of New Testament Christianity and the Gospel of Jesus Christ.

Where was God on Good Friday? God was on the cross, dying for our sins. Where was God on Monday morning? You tell me. God was right there. God was all around.

I admit it, I'm not a Calvinist. While I have a depraved view of humanity, I cannot accept that evil is part and parcel of God's divine plan. To make that assertion means that you must accept that evil is equal to good. It requires the premise that God's power in the world is matched by the power of evil. Listen to how many so called evangelicals and fundamentalists talk about evil. Evil is presented as an equal player in a divine chess match. According to some, God only wins through luck and Satan's ultimate stupidity. It has nothing to do with their convictions about the theological significance of the events of the first Easter Sunday.

I can't accept that. I will not agree that the power of evil is equal to the power of God. I will not accept that we are powerless when it comes to confronting evil. If the crucifixion of teaches us anything, it is that death itself is not barrier to God's reigning and conquering everything in its path.

I believe in free will. Free agents may commit evil actions out of the freedom they've been given. That's how God made us. To be concise, I believe that if God were to 'get involved' (like a puppet master) and start influencing human actions for the better, then human actions would no longer be free. We couldn't make any moral choices, for ill or good. We would be divine playthings. Does that sound like anything remotely related to the message of Jesus Christ? No, it doesn't. So beware. By Friday (or the closer we get toward next Sunday), CNN, Fox, and MSNBC will be trying to put this tragedy into some kind of theological context. They will have the token evangelical who will espouse the deterministic viewpoint. It is doubtful that they will find a middle of the road Protestant or Roman Catholic who isn't a determinist. Those people don't attract viewers or increase ratings. In these situations, ideologues are the voices that are the most often heard.

The writer Kurt Vonnegut died this week at the age of 84. He was one of the great writers of the 20th century. In 1980, he preached a sermon where he said, "People don't come to church for preachments, but to daydream about God."

Vonnegut said Christians don't come to church (or encounter organized religion) to be lectured and instructed about certain facts, but to be open to the possibility of other explanations; explanations that defy our own desires for rational order. I rather like that, and I believe this is true. People don't come to church, to God, to worship to be told the way it is, that evil is something we have to accept-in the same way we accept Jesus Christ as our Lord and Savior. I do not have to accept the ultimate power of evil because I have accepted the ultimate reality of Easter Sunday. People come to church, whether in Russia or Raleigh, to experience Christ personally. There's only so much I can say about faith. To really know the reality of faith, it must be experienced.

People of faith don't come to church to have religion dumped onto their plate by embittered, theologically illiterate spiritual cafeteria workers (i.e. some pastors and lay people both), people come so that as part of a community that seeks to live in a way that runs counter to conventional wisdom and popular culture, we can bring our fears and dreams and needs and joys and our hurts and our praises and our uncertainties, all of it, and in God's presence we find healing and hope and wisdom and strength for the journey. It is not about certainty so much as it is about relationship and about openness to God, a God that we do not fully know and a God that we cannot control.

Killing Christmas

It's been one week since the marathon meeting. I'm not certain that I've recovered. Maybe I have, maybe I haven't.

For many reasons, consistent sleep has been elusive over the past few weeks. That fact was driven home this morning when I arose in the 8 am darkness and stumbled to the bathroom sink. As I reached for the light and looked at the face staring back in the mirror, all I saw were my blood-shot eyes. The eyes said it all. Whether on the train or in my own bed, I haven't had a decent night's rest in several weeks. I thought by now it would get better. It hasn't. Maybe it's the weather or the consistent darkness and lack of sunshine. Perhaps it is all in my head.

Russia is a strange place to celebrate a holiday like Christmas. It's honestly like living in a bizarre alternate reality, where things look similar and familiar but on closer inspection, you realize that nothing is the same. These complex practices, an almost Byzantine web of holiday celebrations, form an olla podrida of folk, religious, secular, and Soviet rituals. This flies in the face of the prevailing wisdom and sweeping generalization that the Soviets took the Christ out of Christmas. To those of you who adopt this as your perennial Christmas culture war issue, you would do well to look into Russia's history.

During the Soviet era, New Year's festivities became the focus of December's celebrations and gatherings. The powers at be realized they couldn't wipe the entire holiday off the map. Instead, they secularized the entire season. In essence, it's like having Christmas without ever mention-ing Christmas. Russians purchase New Year trees instead of Christmas trees. Signs across town wish shoppers and commuters, "Happy New Year" in large font. In a few places, the words "Merry Christmas" are printed in small print. There are no public references to other religious holidays that may fall in December or the New Year season. No one gets bent out of shape at the absence of Hanukah or Kwanzaa celebrations. Children receive "New Year" gifts. You get the picture.

It's important to remember that most Russians still observe some kind of Christmas celebration. Christmas, as the religious holiday celebrating the birth of Jesus of Nazareth, isn't totally absent from contemporary Russian culture. Even during the Soviet period, Christmas was celebrated, though only as a religious holiday within the Orthodox and other underground churches. For that reason, Christmas celebrations have evolved in a slightly different manner than in the United States. Simply because Christmas was removed from the wider consumer driven culture does not mean it was removed from the church or society. There were no public nativity scenes in Soviet Russia but Christmas continued in the churches and homes of believers. There were no Christmas services in schools or concerts on the town squares. Yet, the priest would gather the faithful and say the liturgy each year to remember the birth of Christ.

Here's my point, even though Russia is thoroughly secularized when it comes to our perspective of celebrating Christmas, this secularization has led to a deeper celebration within the Church and lives of individual Christians. The Russians discovered that one doesn't need all of those forced social public observances to maintain the integrity of the Christmas celebration. Those things that many American Christians get angry about each Christmas (removing nativity scenes, saying Happy Holidays instead of Merry Christmas etc...) are truly irrelevant to celebrating and maintaining Christmas traditions. If they were crucial, Christmas would be dead and buried in Russia because those practices were dumped in the mass graves of the Siberian GULAG camps alongside the bodies of countless priests and laypeople. Somehow, even in the face of great persecution, when Christians were being executed, arrested, and condemned for their beliefs, Christmas never died.

If Christmas wasn't killed by the KGB, I don't think we have anything to fear from calls for one less nativity scene or someone else saying "Happy Holidays". Just think, for all the time wasted on those kinds of "moral" issues, people are dying of hunger, freezing to death, and suffering while we have the luxury to debate such frivolities. That can't be right, now can it? That can't be Christian, now can it? Sometimes our Christian priorities are so out of whack; I wonder how we got this far off course.

THE COST OF FREEDOM

As if two hundred years of history wasn't sufficient, Americans have been regularly reminded over the past six years about the cost of freedom. Whether in Iraq or Afghanistan, we have been told to weigh the relative cost of freedom against the unbearable price of failure. (Perhaps this is a sad commentary on how little most Americans understand of their own history. It also reveals how little most people understand about the nature of freedom. I see this now because I live in a place where true political freedom is in short supply.)

Despite grave assertions and complex arguments that find their roots in sources as diverse as Thomas Paine, Abraham Lincoln, and Milton Friedman, there is one aspect of this debate that has been consistently ignored. In Russia's painful transition from Communism to something resembling democracy, freedom and capitalism have spelled the death knell of the free public toilet. Through the halcyon days of Lenin's first five year plan to the shortages of Perestroika and Glasnost, state subsidized sites for self-urination were a gift from the party to the people. Sadly, this is no more. In the era of globalization and free-market economics, urination requires a user fee.

Not long after the hammer and sickle was lowered for the last time from the Kremlin towers, wily entrepreneurs moved in to corner the newly privatized toilet market. With literally thousands of franchise opportunities available across the city, Babushkas who could provide their own cleaning supplies chunked down the license fees and set up shop in Metro stations and parks across the Russian capital. The key to success in the public toilet market is location, location, location. Downtown, near any of the hundreds of bars and cafes, was considered prime real estate. The further one travels beyond the garden ring road the cheaper it becomes to relieve oneself in public.

If you live in Moscow, as I do, this is a reality that one must come to terms with shortly after your arrival. Unlike mastering the complexities of the Russian language, learning the language of finding a toilet after six cups of Russian tea and three Diet Cokes, is not a skill that can be acquired at leisure over a long period of time. Because I know the basic code of the public toilet system, I won't reach for a Diet Coke, a cup of coffee, or a mug of tea without first considering the location and costs of the nearest public toilets. If I expect to be on the metro or the bus an even closer analysis of the toilet situation is required. That is how I live now. Though, it wasn't always this way.

On a cold afternoon, with a shrunken bladder full of Diet Coke, I was standing in the middle of Red Square. Gazing at the entrance to Lenin's tomb, it occurred to me that I would soon need to find a bathroom. In spite all of the gaudy changes in Moscow's architecture; they've still not allowed port-a-johns onto Red Square. The nearest toilets were outside of the square, adjacent to the metro station. As such, I needed to put the socialist nostalgia tour on hold and start heading for home. The problems began soon thereafter. The further I walked the greater the urge became. By the time I reached the Resurrection Gate, I was positively goose stepping across the cobble stones. Despite the simplicity of my plan to walk from the square to the public toilets, I knew it would not be that easy. After all, this is Moscow and nothing is ever easy.

The over priced souvenir hawkers who work just outside the gate will jump on any foreigner they see. Even if you've walked by them fourteen times earlier in the day, they will still approach you and ask if you'd like to buy a large Russian fur hat. As I made my way between the merchants, one man offering both hats and stamps approached me for the third time in as many hours.

"Meester, don't you want to buy hat?"

"No thank you," I said. I was almost running at this point.

"Meester, you need Russian hat." He wouldn't give up that easily.

"No," I yelled. "I don't need another Russian hat. I already have a Russian hat." I didn't want to be rude.

Whether his English was lacking or my Russian was insufficient, I'll never know. Whatever the case, he wasn't getting the picture.

"I'm going to the bathroom," I yelled.

"Hat meester, you want buy a hat?" He wouldn't shut up.

By this time, I was reaching the failsafe point, the crisis moment, the point of no return. I really wanted this guy to leave me alone. It was taking all of my energy to keep my bladder under control, translate between two languages, and search for a public toilet. The nearest toilets were at least fifty yards away. It wasn't clear whether this man was desperate enough to sell a hat that he would follow me into a public toilet smaller than most phone booths.

Hat, you want hat?"

"For God's sake, I don't want to buy one of your damn hats! I just want to pee!" I screamed. Ok, maybe it was a little stronger. It may not have been the most missionary-like thing to say but given the circumstances, the only conversion I was hoping to do was to complete the process of turning Diet Coke into urine. He finally got the message.

"You don't want hat," I heard him say, half in question and half in understanding, as I sprinted onward.

It wasn't really a problem that I still couldn't see the toilets. Before you see the toilets you can smell them. That unique combination of disinfectant and urine emanates in a least a 200 hundred foot radius from the actual toilet. All I had to do was follow the smell. The large Russian woman who operated the toilet (operating consisting of taking money, cleaning it occasionally, and pointing at the door of which toilet the patron is to use) seemed to be asleep. As she was the size of a small Rwandan mountain gorilla, I was cautious not to startle her. I poked her gently on the arm. With a deep grunt and a short moan, she moved from sleep into consciousness. From her expression, I wasn't sure if she was going tear my arms off and use them as clubs to subdue a wildebeest or the hat man.

"I need to use the toilet," I said in my best Russian. That was a phrase I had learned in the Slavic language lab at UNC-Greensboro.

"Fifteen rubles," she said, sticking out her hand.

"Fifteen rubles, it cost fifteen rubles?" I don't remember if I was talking to her or myself.

"Pet-nad-set," she said, clearly enunciating each Russian syllable. After all, I was a dumb American and she wanted to make sure that I understood.

I had no idea one had to pay to pee. Why had no one told me this? I read hundreds of articles and books each year about life in Russia and not one had mentioned a urine tariff. I dove frantically into my pockets. The large LL Bean jacket I was wearing was originally designed for people climbing Mount Everest. To that end, it is packed with pockets galore both inside and out. Where was my money? Where was my change? I recently discovered Russian merchants are unable to make change for anything above a 100 Ruble note (about four dollars). Even if could lay my hand on a 500 Ruble note, she wouldn't change it. At this rate, I was about to have the most expensive urination of my thirty-two short years. I was sure that a 485 Ruble tip was a little above the going rate.

I was now about to burst. In some exotic combination of River Dancing and Cossack folk kicking, I tried to keep continent and find my money at the same time. Eventually, piecing together an array of coins that I was sure must have totaled 15 rubles; I threw them into the woman's paw like hand and moved for the door.

I have a weak gag reflex. Even the memory of the macaroni and cheese meals from my old elementary school can still provoke the dry heaves. You can imagine what this encounter with a Russian public toilet entailed. First of all, it is a stretch to call these facilities "toilets". It's more of a hole, in the ground, over which a plastic booth has been strategically placed. There is nowhere to sit. On some kind of nail, hook, or twig there might be pieces of the cardboard fiber that Russians refer to as "toilet paper".

By now I am trying to control the release of two bodily functions, all without touching anything. Holding my breath and picking a spot on the wall, I remember what they tell people who are afraid of heights, don't look down. I keep repeating to myself, "Richard, whatever you do, don't look down." I'm flying blind. I have to do this without looking at what

I'm doing. Wanting to spend no more time in this Russian gas chamber than needed, nature took over and my dignity, or whatever remained of it, was saved.

That was until I started reading what was on the wall. Like Applebee's or any other sport-bar type places in America, Russians have started to put newspapers and other advertisements in public bathrooms. In high-end restaurants and public toilets you can read the latest hockey scores or see the results of a Ukrainian chemist's quest to cure baldness. I must tell you that even in the best of circumstances, it is difficult for me to pee and do other things at the same time. I can multi-task in most areas of my life yet this is a skill which eludes me.

When you're in a nasty Russian public toilet and suddenly presented with something to read while you wile away the time, let me recommend against the reading, focus on the urination. Reading in a foreign language and urinating in a public toilet both require their own unique forms of concentration. When you're trying to relieve yourself, it is best not to get stumped on a verb that can be easily looked up when you're in the fresh air. It's easier that way. If you break that concentration for even a moment, you can end up spending the rest of the afternoon smelling like a nursing home. Trust me, I know.

The Meeting from Hell

I can't remember when I've been in a meeting that went as long, was as complicated, and tested every fiber of my being. Had it not been for the intensive, multi-year long meeting survival training I experienced as a staff person in a non-profit organization somewhere in the United States, I wouldn't have made it. Then, I was known only as "Number 2". Now, I'm putting that training to use, somewhere in the Union of Soviet Socialist Republics (former). Like NBC News's recent decision to refer to the conflict in Iraq as a "civil war", the creators and editors of Missionary Man have also made an important editorial choice. From hence forth, the former Soviet Union will be referred to as the Union of Soviet Socialist Republics (former).

It was around 9:00 pm when the hallucinations started. At first, they were quite mild. I could see myself floating up from the table, walking toward the door, picking up my bag, and going toward the bus stop. Like an illusion of an elusive desert oasis, it vanished in a moment as someone revived me with a cup of Russian.

It had taken until now for me to stop smarting over comments made about some of my work earlier in the day. I offered a draft document for review that I had originally written in English and then translated into Russian. Apparently, though the Russian was grammatically correct, it seemed to present a problem that, "It didn't sound Russian enough." In fact, it was even said the document, "sounded like it was written by an American." I wonder how that could be! Really, my "tone" didn't sound

Russian enough! It seems my grammar and syntax sound more like an English speaker than a native Russian speaker.

If I were to escape this death by meeting scenario, I would need a cunning plan to debouch from my increasingly feeble mind.

Attracting as little attention as possible, I reached into the left cargo pocket of my pants and found my mobile phone. If I could get to phone, I reasoned, it might be possible to write an SMS text message requesting help with a well timed phone call. That might be enough to get me out of the meeting, if only for a few minutes. After all, if I was receiving late night phone calls in Russia, it must be important and I could at least get up, get out of the room and regain my faculties.

Using my best Western-Union telegraph vocabulary, I typed with my left hand while taking notes with my right. (Missionary Man has a black-belt in multi-tasking.) As best I can recall, the message read as follows:

HELP STOP. IN WORLD'S LONGEST MEETING STOP. CALL ME NOW TO AID IN ESCAPE PLAN STOP YOURS TRULY, MISSIONARY MAN

Next, I accessed my list of contacts and requested that nearly new Nokia phone place each mobile number resting in its expanded memory into the "To:" box. The message would then travel to countries far and wide, greatly increasing the chance of finding someone, anyone who might help me escape from this jam.

The minutes crept forward at the pace of a dying, asthmatic, one-legged snail. The waiting was endless. Seconds turned into unrelenting, unstoppable minutes. I could only guess time would march on; dragging the subsequent minutes toward a further accumulation of hours. I thought, "These are moments of my life I will never regain. They are to be buried here in this small, hot meeting room on the first floor of a former day care center in Moscow. May they Rest in Peace." Tragic, I know.

Just when I was ready to give up, my phone began to ring. "Thank you, God", I uttered in a silent word of praise. The familiar ring of the Nokia 6110 momentarily stopped the Russian participants from yelling at each other. On the third ring, I took the phone from my pocket and said, "I need to take this call."

I got up from my seat and walked to the door, determined to find a bit of fresh air in this, my momentary reprieve. Once I was out the door, I pushed the answer button and said, "Thank you very much." I hadn't looked at the caller id and as such, I had no idea with whom I was speaking.

There was a pause on the line. Then a Russian voice came on and asked (in Russian), "Is Sasha there?"

Not believing my ears, I re-posed the question to the questioner.

"Is Sasha here?"

"Yes," he asked. "Is Sasha there?"

I'm not certain he could hear the disappointment and exasperation in my tired, American sounding version of the Russian language.

"No, Sasha isn't here."

"Oh," he said. "I must have the wrong number."

"Yes, you must have the wrong number."

Then the line went dead.

My head hung low, I shuffled back into the room and was greeted by the same friendly Russian faces I had stared at for the previous 14 hours.

"Who was that?" someone had the nerve to ask.

"Oddly enough, it was the Russian Orthodox Patriarch Alexei II inviting me for dinner and drinks aboard the Patriarchal Yacht, "The Saucy Sioux", currently wintering in the Caribbean with the New Zealand Cricket Team and the Balinese Goddess of Plenty."

Then, as if on some sort of unseen dramatic cue, one of the English speakers asked, "really?"

The Gulf of Finland in January

The villages dotting the Russian landscape north of Moscow are small places. Despite Moscow's ever growing expanse of concrete and glass apartment buildings, most of Russia is still trapped in late 19th and early 20th century rural obscurity. These are the places often referred to as the "real" Russia. Yet, some still maintain that living in a city where government officials and journalists are regularly assassinated is the Slavic equivalent of enrolling at Hogwarts, a good story but not representative of reality.

It was exactly these cities I was traveling through just a few weeks ago as I headed toward St. Petersburg. The geniuses who decided midnight trains arriving at 8:00 am the next day were good ideas have never ridden on their own trains. On paper and in theory, it does sound like a good idea. However, when you step inside the crowded compartment with three complete strangers, one of whom is offering you part of a still flipping fish and a shot of vodka; the good sounding idea dissipates faster than an air horn in a vacuum. Fresh fish at that hour wasn't my idea of the ideal midnight snack. My only desire was to go to bed. My three traveling companions had other ideas. They wanted to chat and share the communal fish. Despite the overt Biblical imagery, my gung-ho desire to recreate the feeding of the five thousand was nowhere to be found.

For at least an hour after we left the station, the overhead fluorescent lights blazed and the cramped compartment began to smell like the overheated back room of an Azerbaijani fish market. My bed was a top bunk thus hotter and even more uncomfortable than those below. Despite these extreme conditions, I was proud that my nausea and gag reflex stayed in check until 3:00am. Fumbling for the door in the dark, I undid the lock after about 10 minutes of trying to find the bolt. My now sleeping neighbors started to grumble as made my way to find fresh air.

It takes a certain amount of talent to vomit on a moving train. A combination of skill, timing, and hand eye coordination are the keys to hitting the hole in the floor. Strictly speaking, there wasn't a toilet. With one hand on placed on each of the narrow walls and my legs about shoulder length apart, I was able to hit the target. Given the oppressive heat of the compartment, I was tempted to bring a blanket into the hallway and sleep there. I knew the conductor wouldn't like it at all. The only alternative was to climb back into my sauna and hope I didn't arrive in Petersburg smelling too much like a fishy drunk.

To be specific, my destination wasn't St. Petersburg. I was heading about 45 kilometers north to a small village called Komarovo. Komarovo is a hamlet situated in the swampy marshland along the Gulf of Finland. Before World War II, it was Finnish territory. After the war, many famous Russian writers and artists moved to Komarovo in order to paint abstract pictures and write extremely depressing poetry. Today its population consists of four dachas, three rather mangy cows, a Dachshund named Colin, and a small hen in her late 40's.

In such an isolated area, it is important to stock up on supplies. My first order of business was to find the one functioning general store. Rumors had circulated across western Russia and Ukraine that it was becoming nearly impossible to find Diet Coke. I wasn't going to make it for three days and two nights without some kind of caffeinated diet beverage. If could also lay my hands on some ketchup, all the better. If the food was palatable, it was possible to bear the worst of Soviet hospitality houses. I once stayed in a place called the Nagorno-Karabakh Industrialization of the Masses Leading to Revolutionary Peace Workers' Guesthouse. The toilets were broken, there were no working phones, and people were regularly stabbed in the bar. However, the kitchen made the best omelets west of Baku. The food in the Komarovo Friendship of All People's Hotel redefined the meaning of bland. In my frantic packing, I had forgotten to grab my travel bottles of ketchup, Texas Pete, and Tabasco sauce. I wasn't hopeful I would find either in Komarovo but I was determined to try.

This wasn't my first trip to Komarovo. I was last there during the early summer months when the mosquitoes return from their annual holiday in Denmark. From my earlier visit, I thought I remembered where to find to the store but in the snow nothing looked familiar. The snow completely changed the entire environment. Without the haze of gnats and mosquitoes, it was difficult to reorient my bearings to the arctic-like conditions of late January.

With a due sense of exhaustion and dread, I set off for the main settlement. Following the train tracks for half a mile, even I found it hard to believe that I was trekking through knee deep snow for one bottle of ketchup and six cans of Diet Coke. My actions were those normally associated with people in the clutches of heroin addiction. Was I addicted to Diet Coke and ketchup? By all objective standards, this made no sense at all.

Turning right at the train station, I crossed the tracks and headed into the town. The place seemed entirely deserted. There were no signs of life in any direction. Remember the deserted town in the movie Kelly's Heroes? If you take away the tank and add several feet of snow, that's what it was like. Where were the people? Were they all dead? Had bird flu ravaged the village and Russian government tried to cover it up? Had I missed the rapture? That would be my luck. I didn't know what was going on.

To the best of my knowledge, there were two shops in Komarovo. One was a smaller place carrying bottles of vodka, a traditional drink known as vodka, and travel size containers of vodka. The second place was a grocery store in the more conventional sense of the word. They carried an assortment of light bulbs, vodka, sausages, vodka, screwdrivers, vodka, cigarettes, and Schweppes cranberry juice. It was in this second shop I thought I might find some cola. I kept turning right. I remembered that the place was behind a Russian body shop. About the time my extremities were growing numb and starting to turn black, I rounded the corner, saw the body shop and located the store.

From the moment I walked in the door, it was clear the clerks and the four other shoppers realized I was from out of town. I could tell from their wary glazes and suspicious glances they immediately pegged me as a foreigner. As I had come seeking only ketchup and diet cola, I wanted to allay their fears.

In most traditional Russian grocery stores, the products are kept behind a counter. You can't go to an aisle, pick up your goods, and check out. First, you've got to get the attention of the clerk. This is often the most difficult part of shopping. Russian clerks do not naturally ask waiting customers, "Can I help you?" If, by chance, they do notice you waiting, they might say, "I'm listening." That's your cue to jump in and state your request. It is also recommended that you know exactly what you want to purchase. They have little patience for confused or uncertain shoppers. Imagine a whole culture of food retailing based upon the Soup Nazi's customer service practices. That's shopping in Russia.

With all of this in mind I asked, "Would any of you female clerks (a standard term in Russian) be able to help me purchase some food products?" That's what I thought I said. What they heard was a little different. I actually said, "I am not here to take your women, buy property, or genetically modify your Cola." As a foreigner in a strange village that was deemed to weird for the Russian version of the Twilight Zone, this wasn't a good way to find Diet Coke or ketchup. I decided to try another approach.

"Do you have cola light and ketchup?" I asked. I thought simpler was better.

"You mean together?" she said.

"No, I mean cola light (the Russian term for Diet Coke). I also want to purchase a bottle of ketchup."

"Oh," finally acknowledging her understanding.

"No, we don't".

"Do you have any Pepsi Light?" I asked.

"Yes," she said.

"Can I have that then?"

"Yes, but I thought you wanted cola light?"

"I did, originally, but Pepsi Light will suffice."

She ducked below the counter and pulled out one small bottle of Pepsi Light.

"Could I have two others please?"

After dramatic search of the rear storeroom, she returned with two additional bottles of Pepsi Light. This didn't bode well for my second request. I knew they had ketchup. I had seen it in the deli case beside the dog food when I came in.

"What kind of ketchup do you want?"

"Whatever you've got is fine?" I said.

The clerk went to the end of the counter and pulled out a bottle of St. Petersburg's own "Admiral" brand. It would have to do. At this point in my expedition, all I wanted was to take my Pepsi, Ketchup, change, and go back to where I was staying. I laid 57 Rubles down on then counter, asked her for a plastic bag (those aren't standard in most Russian grocery stores), and made my way for the door. If a lynch mob had formed and was waiting for me outside in the parking lot, I had little chance of making it back alive. I didn't want to offend these people any more than I had already. It was time to leave.

"Professor Richard, can I ask you a question?"

Words that can stop even the most confident ESL teachers dead in their tracks! I always treat such queries with a degree of trepidation when they originate from members of my ESL Class. However, it is a door I have opened and can't complain when the students decide they want to walk through. At the end of each class, we have a question and answer time where the students should be posing questions about English grammar but invariably they end up asking about life in America. It is possible at times like this to observe the latent effects of Soviet propaganda still circulating among average Russians.

Earlier in the class, I asked the students to read a short story they had written using the previous week's concept (present continuous) and vocabulary words. After an opening saga about a cheese eating and olive loving but lonely Bigfoot who moves in with a Russian man who lives in a haunted hut, I was open to answering questions on about any topic under the non-existent Russian sun. However, I was pleased they remembered two important facts about my own culinary tastes (a sincere disdain of olives and cheese) from a previous week's class on communicating likes and dislikes.

"Sure, you can ask me a question."

"I have heard that there are very small white people in America."

"Come again?"

"I have heard there are very small white people in America. Is this true?"

I didn't know quite how to respond. So I took a stab in the dark. But before I realized what was starting to come out of my mouth, I asked, "Are you asking if there are Albino midgets in America?"

She stared at me blankly. I realized my politically incorrect faux-pas and adjusted accordingly. "Are you asking if there are vertically and pigment challenged people in America?"

The blank look became blanker. I could tell she was thinking of another way to phrase her question.

"Yes," she said. "I have heard there are small white people in America. Is this so? Are they discriminated against?"

"You've heard right," I said. "There are a number of vertically challenged albinos living in the United States. There are also dwarfs who aren't Albinos. They refer to themselves as 'little people'. Often times, they are able find work in television or the circus." I couldn't provide much in the way of statistics or other details about the lives of albino dwarfs. I hoped she would take my word.

"No, no, no!" she says.

"Oh, boy," I thought. Had I offended her? Were her parents "little people"? She probably wrote her dissertation at Moscow State on the problems of dwarfs in the American circus industry. What had I led myself into?

"I have heard there are more black people in America than white people."

"Oh," I finally realized what she was asking.

"No, I don't think there are more African-Americans than Caucasians in the total population. In some places, that may be the case but on the whole that's not an accurate statement."

It is important to remember that the Soviets painted an extremely negative picture of life in the United States. They viewed their own crumbling amoral empire as the prototypical society of the future. America was a land rife with drugs, plagued by crime and racism. Sadly, that is still the image many Russians people have of modern American life. Luckily, after seventy years of Communism and fifteen years of something called "freedom", I had arrived to set the record straight. Just when I think things can't get much stranger, weirdness rears its misshapen Slavic head; an albino dwarf grabs the wheel of my well-ordered life and drives into the mountains for a dinner engagement with cheese eating, olive popping Bigfoot.

Dante's Hell

I learned from CNN this morning about another major snowstorm affecting the northeastern United States. Schools are delayed, roads are closed, and the even Federal government is opening on a two hour delay. It must be bad. Some places in upstate New York have received more than ninety inches of snow. How do people live in such places? I'll never know how they cope with the excessive cold and snow.

Those long train rides give one much time to think. As I was riding back from St. Petersburg a few weeks ago, watching the snowy landscape from the train window, I began to fixate on the snow. If I've learned anything over the past year, it is that snow doesn't stop traffic, ground flights, or make normal life impossible in Russia. Another major difference between the epic snow storms of the northeast United States and Russia is Russians receive snippets of snow spread across many months; big American snow storms dump feet of snow in a concentrated period of time. Russians also have centuries of experience in dealing with snow and extreme weather. The snow becomes the background to life, rather than something defining major aspects of life.

For ordinary Russians, the snow is simply "there". I have begun to realize at this point in the winter, I'm starting not to notice the snow. It is so ubiquitous; it is almost possible to forget it is still there. I said almost possible. It is at least until I fall asleep. On many nights I have found myself dreaming about the spring. I've dreamt of blue sky, warm temperatures, fresh air, and green grass. How I do crave air free from second hand smoke! It is when I wake up from that dream and look out the window at the snow covered sidewalks I remember the unavoidable reality of the snow.

Snow is one of the most common realities associated with life in Russia. If people know nothing else about this country, they know it is both cold and snowy. When people think of Russia, they think of snow. In fact, if one were to ask 99 of 100 people how often it snows in Russia, they would say "all year". I know people who believe this place is like Superman's Fortress of Solitude, perpetually frozen in ice. So much so that the first question I am regularly asked by friends and family is, "So is it cold over there?" I am tempted to say, "No, it's actually quite balmy." The idea of Russia as one large, snowy, frozen GULAG camp was part of an extensive CIA propaganda campaign designed to make the Soviet Union look bad to sun worshipping Americans. You know I'm kidding, right? Or am I?

After six weeks of nothing but snow, it does become hard to imagine anything different. As attractive as the Superman metaphor might be to myself and my work, it doesn't quite do it for me. Instead, I prefer to think of Russia's environment with a different image: Dante's Inferno. As Virgil and Dante come to the end of their journey through the underworld, they arrive in the 9th circle of Hell. With the help of a giant named Antaeus, they are deposited on the edge of a massive frozen lake, a place called Cocytus. In Dante's vision of Hell, the lowest and worse level isn't a place of fire and flame, it is a frozen wasteland. The damned are condemned to stand up to their necks in the frozen lake. Their tears form blocks of ice hanging from their faces. At the center, a three headed Lucifer stands waist deep in the frozen water. In each of his three mouths, he continually devours the three greatest betrayers in history: Judas Iscariot, Marcus Brutus, and Caius Cassius. In case you forgot, the last two killed Julius Caesar.

Hell as a frozen, barren wasteland. Laying aside the arguments about "literal" and "figurative" Hell, Dante's image rings true. Maybe the vast frozen expanse of Russia is a kind of Hell. If it is, I guess I'm a missionary in Hell. As strange as that sounds, given the needs here, what better place to be a work?

The Foreboding Gray

Damn this godforsaken grayness! I don't mind the cold. The pitch black darkness at four o'clock in the afternoon couldn't bother me in the least. Night is night. Dark is dark. That doesn't faze me. I don't even mind the snow. I am, however, growing to mind the monochrome, black and white world that seems to know no end. While this has been the warmest December and November since Nicholas II was the Czar, the warmth has done little to relieve the cloud cover and lack of sunshine. Enough of my existentialist meteorology!

The people who ride the public buses never cease to fascinate me. So much so, I wonder if they are the remnants of some lost Israelite tribe. This particular morning, I was waiting at the bus stop of the apocalypse when all four horsemen arrived at the same time. Because it is an exceptionally small shelter, I was forced to scoot over to make room for them as well as their horses. Let me assure you, it was quite cramped.

While we waited, I was able to ponder this question. Why do they remind me of an Israelite tribe? Because, like our desert wandering ancestors, the Muscovite bus riders can turn angry and virulent in a moment's notice when things don't go their way. The drivers, far from being a semi-benevolent Semitic deity, are given the task of bearing most of this hostility. What, might you ask, drives these elderly women (mostly) to hurl obscenities that would make even the saltiest sailor blush? The drivers have this funny habit of insisting people purchase tickets to ride the bus. Imagine that! They actually want people to purchase a ticket before sitting down in a seat. Apparently, this is too much for some elderly Russians to bear.

Ignoring the fact that Russian pensioners are provided with free monthly bus passes, it seems too much for them to actually obtain a ticket then present the ticket when attempting to board the bus. In this near daily theatrical production of This Absurd Russian Life, here's how the scene typically unfolds:

"Excuse me, you need to swipe your ticket," says the driver.

"Ticket," asks the babushka. She says this is in such a way that suggests she has never heard of something called a "ticket". Tickets, what are they? Buses, you mean this thing I'm riding on is called a bus? Tickets are regarded with the same degree of importance for riding Moscow buses in much the same way as the vows of fidelity are in French marriage services.

"Yes," the driver says again, "you need to swipe your ticket." Again that word, "ticket". You would have thought she was just asked to explain the theory of relativity to Stephen Hawking's voice synthesizer.

"Oh, I don't have a ticket," says the pensioner.

"You need a ticket," the driver reminds the woman.

"Do you not know that pensioners ride for free?" the babushka asks like an attorney in the midst of a difficult cross-examination.

"Yes, I know." "I also know you still need a free ticket in order to ride."

This is when the trouble really begins. The bus driver has picked the single straw that has broken the babushka's back. It is not enough that the driver had the gall to ask for a ticket. Now this insolent young person (probably in their 50's) has actually suggested she actually go and get the free ticket.

"I lived through two world wars and Communism and you're going to make me pay for a bus ticket," the woman yells at the driver.

"We're not making you pay for a ticket," screams the driver.

"It's free, you just need to go and pick it up."

While I am certain the driver and everyone else on the bus respects the efforts these babushkas made toward defeating Nazi Germany and ending Communism, it seems a little much that they couldn't simply pick up their free ticket.

These ticket incidents, or variations of them, are not the most hateful scenes played out each day on Moscow's trolley buses. No, the most anger is reserved for a driver who refuses to open the doors of the bus until the bus is stopped at the official bus stop. Often, the traffic leading toward the major bus stops (those at Metro stations) is backed up for more than a block. Drivers will (though they aren't supposed to) open the doors before the actual stop to let people exit the bus. In fact, I've ridden the number 28 route enough now to know which drivers will and won't let you off early.

This is a city built on the concept of delay. Moscow is a maze of one way streets, dark alleys, and eight lane roads that double as parking lots. It takes an hour to go anywhere in Moscow and that is if there is no traffic or the subways are only moderately full. Delays happen everywhere. If I've learned that lesson after ten months, one would think the life-long residents of Moscow would know it as well.

Yet, if the bus driver is determined to follow the policy set forth by the Moscow Transit Authority and not open the door before the stop, these elderly women and men gathered by the doors will begin to yell, "Open the door, you idiot!" "Idiot" may be the nicest word I've heard used to attract the driver's attention. Because this is a family friendly book, I can't relate some of the other more direct language employed by these rotund Russian grandmothers.

It makes no sense. Their actions defy all logic, reasoning, and common sense. I guess they think if they are insulting enough, the driver will be forced to acquiesce to their demands. If it doesn't happen after the initial verbal assault, they'll start to wail like people trapped in a sinking ship unable to open a hatch door that would enable them to swim to the surface. If you look close enough, you can see the look of frightened, trapped animals in their eyes. For a moment, you might honestly believe the bus is filling with water and we're all going to die. That's how frantic and crazed they sound. Why they are in such a hurry to go and wait somewhere else, somewhere they can't yell at the driver (i.e. on the subway), I'll never know. I'm not sure I want to know.

Selections from an Unwritten Screenplay

By Richard Bryant

FADE IN:

EXT. MOSCOW - DAY- ESTABLISHING

ROLL CREDITS

RICHARD BRYANT SITS DOWN AT HIS COMPUTER

Today, the snow returned to Moscow, though only for a few hours. And since the temperature was above freezing, nothing accumulated. Though I know I'll probably regret saying this come January, it was nice to see the snow. Anything is preferable to this interminable grayness and drizzle.

I hope you're enjoying the ongoing adventures of "Missionary Man". Please, stay tuned, as they say in the television business. You Tube makes it incredibly easy to share videos with a wider audience beyond those who might only read this webpage. My web page and various writings are intended to give readers (and viewers) a glimpse of some of the things I see, the people I interact with, and a general sense of what life is like in Putin's Post-Modern Potemkin village.

Much of what I write is also parody and satire. It is not meant to be taken too seriously. Though I hope the humor and cultural references provide some context for the real life absurdity I experience every day. There is no book, no how to manual, no seminar, to prepare one to do what I do. Sure, we can all talk in vague generalities (i.e. the theory and practice of missions) but to understand the interconnected nature of our world you must see it from an inside perspective. If I see it, you will see it. That's my promise.

Living in this country is like having front row seats to some Franco-Russian absurdist farce (think Godot meets Solzhenitsyn). As a side note, there are two men who sit at my bus stop most afternoons and evenings. They never get on any bus. Yet it is clear they are waiting on someone who is never going to arrive. One of the men is named Vladimir though I know the other isn't called Estragon. If I can give a glimpse of that kind of unfolding drama, albeit in two minute glimpses, I'm going to do it. Gone are the days where missionaries sent in quarterly letters with news that was months old. That may work for some but not for me. If you want to know what I'm doing, what I'm thinking, or what's happening in Russia you can't get any closer to real time updates than right here. So, now you know, and as GI Joe used to say, "knowing is half the battle".

And so, ladies and gentlemen, as the Sport Utility Vehicle of destiny on the railroad crossing of fate stalls in the path of the speeding freight train of doom, and the signalman of time rushes to fetch his digital camcorder, it is time to say goodbye...

(CUE SARAH BRIGHTMAN AND ANDREA BOCELLI)
FADE OUT

Memories of Christmas Past

In a break between warm up burping contests and extra portions of refried beans, my mind drifted to an earlier holiday memory. What would my own past have to do with riding a train full of Russian belchers to Voronezh? This is because after the large portions of holiday meals, many of my family's holiday gatherings devolve into belching and reflections upon the relative merit and quality of one's gaseous eruptions.

I say my mind drifted, though I can't really say for certain. Perhaps I was sleeping or only daydreaming at night. I honestly can't remember now. Maybe the strange old man waiting in my train cabin was the ghost of Christmas not so long ago and he took me on some kind of mythical journey while I was suffering from the lethal combination of anti-depressants, Diet Sprite, and Russian Brussels Sprouts.

I do remember it all seemed so real. In one minute, I was on the train and in the next; I was reliving a recent journey to a large electronics store to look for a digital camera. This particular store had advertised on television and radio how they would, "beat any quote", in order to win business from their competitor's customers. I decided to take them up on their offer and see if they could truly beat any quote.

The lanky, acne covered teenager who was working the camera section came over to see if I he could be of any assistance.

"I saw in the paper that you all would beat any quote," I said. "Is this still true?"

"Yeah, I think so," he replied.

"Do you need to talk to a manager or something?" I asked.

"It depends on if we can beat the quote."

"But I thought you said you could beat any quote?"

"We can," he said again. I realized we weren't getting anywhere. I would have to move the ball down the field if I was going to get anywhere. I decided I would just have to put it out there.

"Well, I have a quote I'd like you to beat."

"Ok," he said with little or no emotion.

For about five seconds, he stood there looking at me. Maybe he was expecting me to take some piece of crumpled newspaper from jacket pocket.

"Would you like to hear my quote or do I need to speak to a manager?"

"No, you can tell me," he mumbled in a slightly frustrated tone.

So, I told him my quote, "He who fights with monsters might take care lest he thereby become a monster. And if you gaze for long into an abyss, the abyss gazes also into you."

"Huh?"

It was clear that he was stumped. I had the feeling he wasn't going to be able to beat this quote.

"He who fights with monsters might take care lest he thereby become a monster. And if you gaze for long into an abyss, the abyss gazes also into you."

"Huh?"

"Yes," I said. "That's Schopenhauer, though I am not sure that is strong enough to win."

"Dude, I think we meant a quote from some other store," he said, finally managing a reply.

"Oh, so Nietzsche doesn't count?" I asked.

My dream ended just as the security guards were asking me to leave.

For me, Christmas has always been built on such memories. On that evening, the reality of the holiday season was a long way from anywhere as we continued our wind powered journey through the dark Russian night. I really didn't have time to wander through the fields of my own nostalgia. Souls needed to be saved. Each gaseous eruption of sin needed to be offered God's Mylanta to cure the devil's perpetual heartburn.

The more I listened and learned about my new found belching comrades, the more I became fascinated by their stories. Just as the Franciscans can tell countless legends of St. Francis's kindness, there seemed to be an endless supply of similar tales concerning St. Bernard the Seemingly Ignorant. Before Bernard the Seemingly Ignorant became leader of the nomadic belchers, he spent much time as a wandering, itinerant, occasionally employed singing soothsayer. (During this time he was known as Bernard the Sometimes Prophetic) He might not have been the most well-known prophet the Middle Ages produced but he managed to leave behind an interesting record. This impressed me. With his great prophetic stature, I thought I might be able to use him as a point of entry when introducing Christianity to the burping faithful. Maybe this unique aspect of Bernard's past could be my guiding metaphor for sharing the Gospel to Bernard's remaining yet ever dwindling flock.

Bernard began his prophetic career with retrospective predictions, many of which later came true. This early success strengthened his prophetic confidence and encouraged him to start predicting the future. However, out of his 963 career predictions, only 37 have been proved correct. 686 are known to be wrong and 240 remain undecided, including his prediction that one day Roman Catholics would have a Polish Pope. (No one had the heart to tell the belchers about that one.)

Some of Bernard's pre-belching prophetic proclamations bordered on the edge of scientific advancements. For instance, examine these mysterious snippets:

I have seen a mentally challenged black water fowl, living in an alternate (yet strikingly familiar) world from our own. In this realm, the duck steps from the edge of a cliff, expecting further pastureland. He loiters in midair, soliloquizing flippantly, until he chances to look down. At this point, the familiar principle of 32 feet per second per second takes over. However, he will not necessarily fall immediately. He may be given the chance to run (on air) back toward the precipice before he begins to accelerate downwards. Though, he will not be able to run fast enough, and begins to fall just before his arms can reach the edge and safety.

Nor does he necessarily always accelerate at 32 feet per second per second, but often reaches a high velocity instantaneously. Also, this high velocity causes tidal forces such that his arm stretches (while the rest of him falls) long enough to wave bye-bye.

In this same universe, rabbits can dig a burrow across vast swathes of land, even across a continent, in less than 20 seconds and emerge spotlessly clean.

Despite these truly extraordinary visions, a careful look at his records show an overall 5% prophetic success rate which compares unfavorably with Nostradamus's 33% success rate. Though, we should re-member that Nostradamus did cheat. He artificially inflated his prophetic lifetime statistics by predicting personal matters just seconds away. For example, he was once observed saying, "I am going to pick up this tortoise and kick it over yonder hedge." When seconds later the tortoise was indeed seen flying through the air, he was heard say, "Oh, There it goes, check, good job Nostro!"

The late night was turning into early morning. If I was going to be any good to anyone the next morning, I needed to go to bed. What had I gotten myself into?

On Board the Moscow-Voronezh Express

I should probably back up. I don't think I mentioned why I was traveling to Voronezh. Why does anyone ever purposely choose to go to Voronezh? It's quite simple really. My employer was sending me to the wilds of southern Russia to evangelize and witness among the participants in the All-Siberian Belching Contest. From extensive demographic research, senior church officials determined vast spiritual ground lay untilled among Russia's belchers and burpers. We spent weeks pouring over data from soft drink companies, brewers, and other makers of gas inducing food and drink. Like the rich natural gas fields of Russia's pacific coast, the natural gas brewing beneath Russia's vast untapped human resources could also yield great benefits of spiritual wealth. For some reason, it fell to me to lug thousands of belcher-friendly tracts and the specially ordered "It's Okay to Burp" NIV versions of the New Testament to this bi-annual gathering.

Due to unseasonably cold weather, the contest was moved further west to accommodate western Russia's numerous belchers. Thus, the All-Siberian Belching Contest being held outside of Siberia. All of the newspaper had said this was an important and historic first. In the late 1990's there was a series of brutal reprisal killings as the east and west Russian burping community tore itself apart. For years, the debate raged about who were the most authentic and traditional (or "old-school") burpers. It was only after the personal involvement of Boris Yeltsin and a "Burping Summit" held at a Holiday Inn near the Moscow Airport that the bloodletting ceased. To actually hold this competition west of the Urals was further proof of how far Russia had come since the freewheeling Yeltsin years. Enough gas had finally passed between the cheeks of time to make such an event possible.

Thus, if past history was any indication, it should be an interesting trip. Last year's winner performed a stirring rendition of "Around the Mountain, She'll Be Coming" and rumor had it that this same championship belcher was looking to repeat with a new Russian version of "Constant Sorrow, I am Man of".

To be honest, I was a bit nervous about fitting in with a hundreds of Russian belchers. Would I, as the lone American observer, be able to integrate successfully and witness to the Gospel without appearing to judge the moral character of the Slavic burping community?

Most of Moscow's burping elite were aboard this same train. En masse, the group converged on the combined dining and bar car even before the train left the station. Because I nearly missed the train, I wasn't able to pick up a Diet Coke before boarding. As such, I was forced to ask the ancient Mayan eclipse maker posing as a conductor for directions to the dining car to find some caffeinated carbonated beverage. I wasn't looking to pick a fight with a group of rowdy belchers on a late night train. Ordering anything remotely carbonated would draw their attention. If I wanted a Coke, I would have to be subtle and confident.

Making my way to the dining car, I felt as conspicuous as a visually-impaired polar bear trying to gain admittance to a Giraffe's only golf club. Surely, I thought, these championship burpers would be able to spot a missionary only posing as a belching professional. Yet, if I could successfully manage this first infiltration, my subsequent work on arrival in Voronezh might be made all that much easier. It was worth a try.

In all of my days, I had never witnessed such an intimidating yet somehow intriguing sight. Maybe that's not entirely accurate. The bar scene from the first Star Wars movie was both intimidating and intriguing. However, in that case, I was only a passive observer. Then there was that lodge meeting of the West Moscow Guild of Village Idiots.

It seemed that dozens of pairs of eyes were on me as I made my way slowly across the weaving room. Where ever I turned, large Russian men and the occasional woman were drinking cola, beers, and eating exotic Mexican bean based dishes. In a casual conversation with a Belarusian belcher while waiting to board, I discovered that this train's chef was famous Georgian guest worker (trained in Mexico) brought to Russia for the express purpose of preparing these gas inducing meals. These people took their journeys to the competitions as seriously as the competitions themselves. One has to respect that kind of devotion to their art.

Though I didn't know it at the time, the good folks at Pepsi were corporate sponsors of the event. As such, there were no Coke products to be found anywhere on the train. I would have to settle for Pepsi Light or 7-Up. I tried not to look too shocked or startled when this information was revealed. A slip-up like that could have dealt an early and fatal blow to my chances at gaining the trust of the assembled belchers.

"Only Pepsi products, you say," I said in the most nonchalant manner I could manage.

"Aye," said the grizzled bar keep. "It's either Pepsi or nothing at all."

"Then Pepsi it is, my good man. I will have one Pepsi Light and one 7-up please."

I reasoned that at least two highly carbonated beverages should reveal me to be a serious belcher. Three might have been better but again, given my size in comparison to the girth of those surrounding me; I didn't want to sound like I was trying to burp above my weight.

Were I to survive the next long, loud, and smelly eleven hours, I knew that I would never have to prove my missionary credentials again.

The Day after Yesterday

It was the best of times, it was the worst of times, and it was the Renaissance of Russian of Burping. The dark ages of the Soviet past were long gone. A new day had dawned for these near forgotten victims of Communist repression. It may come as no surprise but professional belchers are a competitive lot. Like Bass fishermen, Snooker players, and Elvis impersonators their hobbies become their lives. One could only live upon one's burping laurels for a limited amount of time. There was no time to rest. Just at the instant one realizes you've surpassed all previous time and volume records, along comes someone younger and quicker who can match your best efforts after only a teaspoon of diet tonic water.

As such, Russian burpers are the most paranoid expectorant artists plying their trade today. This has not always been the case. Legends tell of a cult of Hindu belchers who worship a Ganesh (the Elephant god) like deity who knows the secret for burping fire from both trunk and tail. They too are incredibly paranoid at keeping this method of belching secret. Many have died to both protect and reveal this ancient knowledge. Though, a team of English anthropologists have argued quite convincingly that the secret lies in the unique curry recipes found in the Tamil Nadu region.

Again, I should probably back up. Maybe the waning weeks of 2006 were not the defining days of Russian belching. Admittedly, one is always keen to view one's own era as the pinnacle of historical achievement. Though on this particular evening, it was hard to imagine a more glorious past when I was surrounded by the current pantheon of Russian belchers. From my vantage point, I could see Ivan the Terrible (from Novgorod), Peter the Great (from Moscow), and Montague the Mild (a French immigrant from Murmansk). Each of them was a legend, in their own right, within the larger Slavic belching community. It was almost more than I could handle to realize I was riding with these gods among mortals in a cramped Russian railway car en route to the most important event in their annual performing calendar.

Riding along in the lonesome railway car that evening, the air was as alive and as thick as clotted cream that's been left out by some hapless clot until the clots were so clotted up they couldn't be un-clotted with an electric de-clotter. Yes, legends die hard in the thick winds of the burping past. With each new gaseous eruption, every new belch brought to life the epic tales of eruptions long ago. As I listened to the stories while the contestants consumed even more 7-Up and refried beans, Boris the Belarusian reminded the participants of the greatest burping legend of all.

"When Leia was Princess of Austro-Hungary, Bernard was Queen of Estonia, and Morris Dancing was embraced by Blacksmiths everywhere-there roamed a great tribe of nomadic minstrel burpers who inhabited the forests of the western Slavic steppe. Led by a former monk named Bertram the Seemingly Ignorant, (who had escaped from the Budapest Colony for Belchers with Brain Leprosy) they were cast from village to village because of their oral flatulence and exceptionally poor singing ability. Rampant discrimination forced them to live on the margins of an already marginalized society. In towns up and down the Vistula and the Volga Rivers, drug-dealing, cross-dressing, Bubonic plague infected, Visigoth prostitutes were embraced with open arms while these gaseous nomads were forced to beg for food and break wind beyond the city walls. This was a strange era of great portents throughout Europe. A horse had been elected pope in

Avignon and strange prophecies foretold of a great insurrection, coming up from the bottom, and beginning in France. (Though, this was later interpreted as the nationwide consumption of garlic éclairs and not the work of belching revolutionaries.")

As Boris went on, I noticed it was then and only then, when the burping legends were retold, that silence reigned. For those few minutes, no sounds (other than that of the occasional mournful sob) of any kind came forth or smells emerged throughout the entire train.

By this time, we had been heading south for about two hours. At this rate, I knew it was going to be a very long night indeed. We were only getting started.

Living in Byzantium

What does Athens have to do with Jerusalem?

Tertullian

How does one work in a culture where society's perception of religion is shaped by a late 14th century understanding of the church and 19th Century Marxism? It goes without saying, Russia isn't the west. To be more specific, Russia isn't the United States, southern, middle-class, or historically Protestant. That presents a problem. It's a problem because most (if not all) of our models of mission and evangelism are based and rooted in the cultural assumptions inherent within American, southern, middle-class, and historically Protestant Christianity.

The dominant theories, ideas, methodologies, and the evangelical emphases are essentially written to work in one kind of culture, in one kind of country, in one kind of place, and in one kind of language. Our theologies of mission, outreach, and evangelism are designed to address the spiritual needs of people who look like us, talk us, think like us, share similar problems as we do, and come from essentially the same cultural milieu.

It defies all logic and reasoning to think that the plethora of resources available to United Methodists in the United States offering plans for evangelism and church growth have any applicability in a religious culture that is as foreign to western Protestants as can possibly be imagined. Is this the beginning of an apologia against evangelism and mission in the former Soviet Union? No, it is not. It is, however, an attempt to draw attention to the realities of mission service and evangelism in the historically Orthodox countries of the former USSR. In order to under-stand what may be a roadmap for Protestants in the USSR, I believe it is crucial for western churches to rethink and retool both their theoretical and practical approaches to missions in Russia.

We must throw the "book" out of the window. Our preconceived notions about Christianity and its role in society are as foreign to most Russians as public feminism was in Taliban-era Afghanistan. So much of what we know and what we take for granted as "givens" when talking about our faith simply have no cultural relevancy in the former Soviet Union. To begin to understand how Russians (and Slavs in general) view Christianity and the church, one must discard our 21st century notions for the 14th century ideas of Byzantine theology and society.

Russia is a religious environment that has never known a reforma-tion. (One could argue that the Soviet era was an "inquisition" but it is best seen as a seventy year pause in Russia's religious development. Essentially, the Russian Orthodox Church began the 1990's in the same doctrinal and theological position as at the beginning of the 20th century.) The enlight-enment had little effect in this country beyond the salons and palaces of St. Petersburg. Orthodoxy has never faced a genuine challenge to its religious dominance by another Christian tradition in nearly two thousand years. I do not regard Marxism as a challenge to Orthodoxy in the same way Protestants challenged Roman Catholics in 16th century Germany.

The Soviet Union may have eradicated wide-spread religious knowledge over seventy years. However, they failed to eradicate the dominant religious culture and attitudes towards faith, belief, and practice. Beneath the glossy surface and the residual traces of Stalinism, lies religious cultures essentially unchanged since the three great Abrahamic faiths arrived on the western Slavic steppe. The casual observer can easily note the many new and old orthodox churches that dot the Moscow skyline. Yet, in the synagogues, mosques, and temples are there too, holding on to traditions that have never died. To paraphrase the Wizard of Oz, we're not in Kansas in anymore.

Beating the Bishkek Blues

I was so used to imagining everything and thinking of everything as it happened in books,
and to picturing to myself everything in the world as I had previously made it up in my
dreams, that at first I could not all at once grasp the meaning of this occurrence.
Feodor Dostoevsky, Notes from the Underground

... I am convinced there are lots of people in Petersburg who talk to themselves as they
walk. This is a town of crazy people. ... There are few places where there are so many
gloomy, strong and queer influences on the soul of man as in Petersburg.'
Feodor Dostoevsky, Crime and Punishment

December 22, 1849

The haggard men on Semenovsky Square were left standing in groups of three while the escort troops and officials assumed their respective positions. After months in the darkness of prison cells, the reflected light from the sun was almost too bright to see anything. Yet, in many ways, this was a reunion.

Some of the men immediately recognized each other. Others were unknown to the vast majority. Most had been part of a group known as the Petrashevsky Circle. The Petrashevsky Circle was one of many pseudo-revolutionary groups in mid-19th century Russia that began to raise political, social, and religious concerns about the shocking conditions faced by most of the poor throughout Russia. A few, like the recently retired Lieutenant, had spent nearly a year on an island in the Neva River just opposite the Czar's opulent Winter Palace. The Peter and Paul fortress had been originally built in 1740 by Peter the Great to defend Petersburg's harbors from attack. Its thick walls also made damp, dank cells for those considered to risky to live among polite society in St. Petersburg. These men, like so many before them, were going to be examples to other would be upper class radicals. They would have to die.

It was almost Christmas, the perfect time for a festive execution. There was nothing that could spread a little Christmas cheer among the Czar's ministers as a firing squad. They felt good; they felt like they had accomplished something, they felt like they were ensuring the divinely ordained lives they were so fortunate to lead. It had snowed the night before and the previous days clouds cleared as quickly as they arrived. The sun shone brightly as the first group of three were led away to be shot. The sound of their steps moving across the fresh snow added a silent drumbeat to an already surreal scene.

A lieutenant colonel of the secret police read out the sentence. "For participation in criminal plans, for circulating a private letter that contained infamous expressions about the Russian Orthodox Church and Supreme Authority and for an attempt to disseminate writing against the government by means of a hand printing press you are sentenced to be put to death by the firing squad."

In the second group, the man waited with the others as the first were taken forward and offered the traditional blindfolds. The commanding officer gave the order for the troops to load their muskets and take aim. At that moment, a messenger arrived on horseback from the palace bearing a letter from the Czar.

Instead of death, recently court-martialed Lieutenant Feodor Dostoevsky would be sent to the farthest reaches of Siberia. First to a prison in Omsk and then to the 7th Siberian Regiment, guarding the frontiers of Russian expansion among the newly conquered Kyrgyz tribes.

He had written infamous (the 19th century word for defamatory) things about the Russian Orthodox Church and its Patriarch. He had disseminated information critical of the Russian government. I had done the same. Some may argue I haven't stopped. Instead of a hand printing press I am using the World Wide Web. I had been spared death. By Russian standards, of any era, I was lucky to be alive.

Having inadvertently trailed Dostoevsky from the Peter and Paul Fortress, through Semenovsky Square, to the edge of the Kyrgyz steppe, and finally back to Moscow, I saw once again time has passed but Russia remains essentially unchanged. Petersburg is still a somewhat gloomy place haunted by the ghosts of revolutions past, present, and future. It is a place where people talk to themselves, albeit on cell phones. The immense mass of land dividing Russia's east and west is too much to fathom. Each side, as in Dostoevsky's day, remains as disconnected and unaware of each other as they have ever been. In those vast empty miles between his would be place of execution and a village of 10,000 Kyrgyz and Tartar Muslims, lay more answers and even more questions. One trip to Kyrgyzstan would never be enough. Even before I left I knew I would be coming back.

Burana Bound

You ever get ill at ease? About what? I don't know. About anything. Just ill at ease. Sometimes. If you're someplace you aint supposed to be I guess you'd be ill at ease. Should be anyways. Well suppose you were ill at ease and didn't know why. Would that mean that you might be someplace you wasn't supposed to be and didn't know it?
-Cormac McCarthy, All the Pretty Horses

It will not surprise anyone to learn the main road out of Bishkek is only two lanes. The sole route out of the capital leads east to Lake Issyk-Kul and eventually the Kazakh border. I wasn't going that far today. Only about an hour and a half down the road was one of the most historic landmarks in Kyrgyzstan, the Burana tower. If you're ever in the neighborhood and looking for Burana, drive east from Bishkek. The road is straight, no turns, no hairpin curves, really not much different from driving though little towns in eastern North Carolina. However, there is one major difference. Where every little town in North Carolina has at least one Baptist church, these villages all have at least one mosque.

When you get to Tokmok, a fairly large settlement that's hard to miss, you're going to want to turn right at the MIG fighter plane mounted in the first (and only) traffic circle in Tokmok. There is still a Russian military base nearby and Tokmok did have that semi-seedy feel of military towns throughout the world. Pawnshops and tattoo parlors were wedged between auto repair stores and fruit stands. If your guide is driving any-where near the speed limit, you may actually see the sign saying "Burana 12 km" just before the turn. Even if you've seen the sign and followed the directions clearly, you're still going to feel like you're heading in the wrong direction. For not long after making the right hand turn at the MIG you realize you are officially out of town. The village drops slowly away through the rearview mirror and in no time at all, you begin to question the wisdom of the directions you received prior to leaving Bishkek only an hour earlier. At least I did.

My driver stopped twice to ask directions from random strangers walking down the road. They all seemed to point in the general direction we were heading. I don't know whether it comforted me or made me more nervous when they all ended their directions with the same words, "you can't miss it." I was missing it. I couldn't see it anywhere. In terrain this flat, I expected an 80 foot tower to be the most visible object for miles. After our second directional stop, I noticed a set of what looked like very small buildings off to the right. Could this be Burana? I didn't see a tower but maybe I didn't know what to look for. The only picture I'd seen of Burana was in a Soviet-era post card three days earlier.

After speeding by the road leading to these tiny buildings, I convinced the driver to back up and take the path (paths are called roads in Kyrgyzstan) toward the tiny buildings. Who knows, maybe the Burana tower was just a model of some ancient city that once stood on these grounds. I was surprised at the quality of the road, even for Kyrgyzstan. This is one of their major tourist attractions, surely they would have tried to do something about such a worn out wagon track trying to pass muster as a road. This couldn't be right. It was then that one of my traveling companions realized we had taken a wrong turn. This wasn't the road to Burana and we weren't looking at a scale model of some ancient city. This was an

Islamic cemetery complete with near life size mausoleums designed to look like mosques.

"Stop the car!"

"What?"

"This is an Islamic burial ground. We don't want to be driving though their sacred burial ground if we want to get home with our lives." I might have been yelling. I can't quite remember.

I could see the headlines, "Methodist Missionary Lynched for Desecrating Sacred Islamic Burial Site in Central Asia."

In a country most of us have never heard of, Richard Bryant, a United Methodist Missionary drove a 1996 Volkswagen GTI through one of holiest sites in Kyrgyz Islam. When asked what led to this catastrophe, Bryant could only respond with the words, "I'm just looking for a tower."

Slamming on the brakes, he shifted the little red Volkswagen GTI into reverse and began the bumpy ride, albeit backwards, towards the main road. Then up ahead, we saw the sign. The next big road to the right was marked with a sign reading, "Burana". As we made the turn, I saw the unmistakable silhouette of the tower coming into view from behind a grove of trees.

Somewhere inside me, from a place I couldn't name, a voice was telling me that something wasn't right. Surrounding me on all sides were jagged volcanic peaks, endless prairies, and land stretching out for miles to what is, even at the beginning of the 21st century, the very limits of western civilization. By all accounts, I thought I should be taking in the view and relishing the opportunity to see such grandeur. But there is a line, an almost imperceptible demarcation, which divides a sincere appreciation for

creation's intricacies from environmental emotional overload. The mountain peaks were not majestic. They had moved beyond majesty to dread
inspiring monoliths. These cliffs were intimidating crags of volcanic Earth
as deadly as they were pulchritudinous. Standing at the foot of the Burana
tower, I surveyed the vast faultlessness of creation lining the landscape
across the western horizon and realized this was simply too beautiful for
mortals to observe.

I could imagine living in country like this, where distances are
measured in days of travel on foot and horseback rather than minutes in a
car, would have a profound effect on how one might view the world. For
some, it be would be liberation. For others, the mountains would form an
impenetrable fence, creating a forced labor camp of the mind, where escape
and death are the only constant realities, yet indistinguishable from each
other.

Whatever the ancient people who lived here saw in the world
around them, they saw it in terms far starker than those who lived in the
neighboring villages even today. The lives of these people were, to paraphrase Thomas Hobbes, "nasty, brutish, and short." Small, crescent moon
shaped graves were arrayed like stepping stones linking the village to the
tower and then to the mausoleum. If you were going to pray in the
mosque that stood where the minaret stands today, you had to pass
through, what the locals called the "garden of the dead". If I was going to
climb to the top of the tower standing watch over this valley, I was going
to have to make my own journey through the "garden of death" and hope
it wouldn't be my last.

In the distance, flat thunderhead clouds were beginning to gather. If I was going to make it to the top of the tower before the rain set in there was no time to waste. The only way up was by a nearly vertical climb, in total darkness on the rotting rungs of a medieval ladder. I'm usually not the claustrophobic type. I realized to attempt this climb, it would be important to block out my surroundings and keep moving forward.

"Just keep moving" became my mantra and I repeated this over and over as I begin the slow ascent. In some ways, it felt like crawling headfirst into a long, stone sleeping bag. It was impossible to move left or right. It was either keep crawling upward or start falling backward. As the local hospital in Bishkek didn't accept my insurance plan, I decided that going up slowly was better than coming down quickly.

As I inched my way upward, I was asking myself questions. The questions helped distract me from the total darkness and my encroaching fear. Was this land incredibly fertile? No, not really. Were the mountains rich in natural resources and minerals? Somewhat, but aren't all mountains. Unless Genghis Khan, Tamerlane, and Stalin thought beauty was worth fighting and dying for, why on Earth had something so perfect been the scene of such carnage throughout history?

Curbing My Bishkek Enthusiasm

Stultus est sicut stultus facit

-Forrestus Gumpus

I hesitate to call Bishkek a beautiful city. You can't call it beautiful in the same way you would Prague or Vienna. Despite the Soviet architecture, pot holes, decay, and general post-Soviet disorder Bishkek retains an almost indescribable and intrinsic beauty. The first thing I noticed was the how green everything appeared. There were trees and lots of them. There were wide sidewalks lined with grass and trees. These are all rare commodities in most sections of Moscow. Moscow is an urban jungle. Bishkek felt more like a real community rather than a sprawling impersonal metropolis.

"It so green," I remarked to Oleg.

"Yes," he said with obvious pride. "At one time, we were the second greenest city in the whole of the former Soviet Union."

Did he say the second greenest city in the city in the Soviet Union? Here, in the middle of what was semi-arid land, Soviet urban planners had made the second greenest city in the USSR. How did they make such a judgment? What were the criteria used to determine the verdant qualities of Bishkek's streets? Bishkek was green, far greener than Moscow but it wasn't that green. If this was the second greenest city what was the first?

"I guess that means you're now the greenest city in all of Kyrgyzstan." He looked at me rather blankly. I'm not sure my humor translated well into Russian.

The previous night our little foursome had gone to a café as we drove in from the airport. During one lull in the conversation, I asked what Oleg's wife Julia did for a living.

"I'm a doctor," she said.

"A doctor, what is your specialization?"

"I'm a podiatrist."

"The feet," I said, revealing my deep medical knowledge. But I didn't stop there. I went on a little further.

"I have immense respect for people who work with feet. The feet, you've got to love them. You cannot underestimate the value of taking care of your feet."

What was that I said about not looking stupid upon arrival? If she had been a neurosurgeon I would probably have said something about the usefulness of our brains for cognitive thought and reason. My only hope was that after a night's sleep that I'd be more insightful as we wandered Bishkek's boulevards and byways.

We walked a little further, all the while Oleg pointed out fountains, monuments, and other points of interest in the downtown area. I had asked for a tour of Bishkek's cultural and social history and that's exactly what I was getting.

"So what was the greenest city in the former Soviet Union?" I had to know.

"Chisinau, the capital of Moldova."

I could see that. Moldova is in the Carpathian mountain range and is indeed very green. It is on the western most border of what was once the USSR. It's also the one former Soviet republic that is easiest to overlook when trying to remember and name all fifteen. Quite a contrast, I thought, that the first and second greenest cities were on the opposite ends, the eastern and western frontiers of what was once the biggest country on Earth.

It is possible to walk from one end of the downtown area of Bishkek to the other in about twenty minutes. Whether on foot, in a taxi, or in a minibus the typical answer to the question, "how far is it?" is never more than twenty minutes. You can be anywhere in the city in twenty minutes. After the first twenty minutes of my walking tour, we had walked though a variety of sculpture gardens, seen some of the ever present monuments to the "Great Patriotic War", a library or two, and one ice cream stand. The closer we drew toward the town center, the street corners grew busier and more crowded. At each of the larger intersections we passed drink stands where a woman was selling cups and some kind of cold beverage from two large coolers. It was hot and I must have looked thirsty because they noticed me staring at the coolers.

"Would you like to stop and get a drink?"

"Sure, a diet coke would be nice."

"Would you like to try one of these?" Julia asked, pointing to the women with the coolers.

"What are they?"

"It's some of our national drinks."

Remembering that I had asked to see real Kyrgyz culture and the consumption of national beverages falls broadly into the category of experiencing culture, I could give only one answer.

"Yes," I said. I always love to try whatever fermented goat's milk or liquid bread concoction that has been sitting for God knows how long on this street corner in Bishkek.

"Yes, please!"

Ten minutes later, when my vomiting stopped, we turned toward Bishkek's central square. I noticed the rampant new construction. Brand new buildings, recently renovated shops, and new stores were going up and opening everywhere. Maybe one of these new department stores had mouthwash for sale. I could only hope.

Bishkek Beginnings

That's the whole trouble. You can't ever find a place that's nice and peaceful, because there isn't any.

-Holden Caulfield

Before I left for Bishkek, I spent a great deal of time looking at maps. I looked at old maps, new maps, Communist maps, and American made maps of Russia. I have no shortage of maps. It seems that everywhere I turn, whether at my office or at home, I have surrounded myself with maps of Russia. Maybe I have a map fetish? Perhaps "addiction" would be a more apt description. Is it that I am obsessed with direction? Do the maps function as some sort of metaphorical tool in assisting my own personal search for meaning? Well, yes.

My reasons for staring at the maps were quite simple. I was certain whatever it was I was hoping to find was somewhere out there in a place represented on each of those maps. Whether it was printed in 1960 or 2006, each map showed the way between Moscow and Bishkek, Kyrgyzstan. Like Charles Mason and Jeremiah Dixon, I was looking for an indefinable boundary between the known and unknown. Whatever it was, the answer was on the other side of that line.

For my purposes, "out there" was the area beyond the Urals. Anton Chekhov once said that the land before Lake Baikal was prose and everything that came after was poetry. I've never been east of Baikal but I think Chekhov was only partially correct. I believe Russian prose ends where the drama of the Central Asian steppe begins. If European Russia is a narrative and Siberian Russia is a poem then Central Asia must be a drama beckoning a new generation of actors to its old stage.

I knew the answers to my questions must be there somewhere. Unlikely as it may seem, though I was reasonably confident the answers to life's persistent questions were lying undiscovered in Central Asia I wasn't as confident about the questions themselves. I knew where the answers were but I had no idea about the questions they were supposed to answer or the actual content of the answers. Confused? Allow me to explain.

The best question I could come up with was one originally posed by Bruce Chatwin many years ago, "What on Earth Am I Doing Here?" It's one of those all purpose existential questions than can be asked at any time and any place. For instance, if you find yourself standing in a mud puddle eight thousand miles away from home and wonder why you've left a land where there are no mud puddles on public sidewalks, you might ask yourself, "what on Earth am I doing here?". If you come home from work one day after a particularly frustrating eight hours you might ask yourself, "what on Earth am I doing here?"

"Doing" and "here" are existential words which hold a variety of meanings depending on any given situation. I knew what I was "doing". I was doing the work of a missionary. I knew "here" was Russia. However, if I described my work in Russia solely in terms of doing missions, that would be like calling "War and Peace" a little book about Napoleon's invasion of Russia. It may answer the question but it certainly wouldn't tell the whole story. For most of modern history Russians rarely traveled beyond the borders of their local villages. Even in the era of moderniza-tion and collectivization, when Joseph Stalin tried to do what Peter the Great attempted in the 18th century (open Russia to the west), few Soviet citizens were able to travel outside of the USSR. Perhaps this was most visible during the Cold War. If people left, or so the logic went, they wouldn't come back. Travel was reserved for those in the elite or those who could be trusted not defect. The only journeys most Russians could hope to take were those within the borders of their own vast country. Even then, many trips were still out of reach of the ordinary workers. The world was a far away place and no places were farther away that those right here at home. In the darkest days of winter the Russians still had one option for travel, albeit armchair travel, to the vacation hotspots of the former USSR. They could go via postcards. Postcards are very popular in the former Soviet Union. They are not as ubiquitous as they once were but they still hold a place of prominence in helping to tell the stories of the crumbling Soviet past. Why is this? What is it about the postcard? Postcards are usually vibrant images of holiday locations in distant locales. They offer the ideal picture of a far way destination that is rarely obtainable by the average photographer. They are meant to convey in a brief verbal and visual synopsis the essence of any given location. As one Russia collector told me, "Soviet postcards were meant to make you believe that the unreality of the grainy black and white photographs was as real as the snow strewn streets".

During the Soviet era, it seemed every town and city throughout the USSR had its own pack of postcards depicting the social and cultural life of their town. Wrapped neatly in a glossy cover, these cards (sometimes in color but more often in black and white) offered a visual tour of Sochi's beaches, Lenin's places of exile in Siberia, Chekhov's house south of Moscow and on and on. Each year, cards would be printed to advertise the diverse cultural offerings of the republic capitals. If you wanted to know what Kiev, Baku, Tbilisi, Yerevan, or even Bishkek (then called Frunze) was like it was all there in the cards. In many of the antique markets in Moscow, one can find the collections of postcards meticulously preserved and for sale. Collectors will journey from far and wide to peruse box after box of Soviet postcards.

There is one man at the main Moscow flea market that has one of the largest collections I've seen. He also sells antique Soviet propaganda posters but tells me that his best business has always come from the post cards. It seems tourists like me buy the propaganda posters and his Russian clientele are drawn to the postcards. Most of these postcard packs were produced from the mid 1950's until the 1970's. The postcards capture snapshots in time that few Americans have ever seen. They show places in the Soviet Union westerners could not visit until after the fall of Communism. They also show what Soviet cities and towns looked like before the intrinsic social and civic decay began to creep across the Russian landscape.

The day before I left Moscow I found myself leafing through post-card packs. After only a few minutes of searching I came across several sets describing the city once known as Frunze but now called Bishkek. You could see the snow-capped mountains in the background and the gleaming white marble of the standard issue post-Stalinist government buildings and offices. Vintage Volgas were parked on every street. Smiling Kyrgyz and Russians walked hand in hand past the massive Lenin Museum in the central square. Even as late as 60 years ago, the Moscow authorities wanted to make an unmistakable point about their presence in Central Asia: bigger is better, bigger means powerful and power means permanence.

Forty eight hours on from looking at those post cards, I was sitting in the back of a minibus taxi, seeing those same mountains and buildings. The postcards were now a three dimensional reality, in living color, and they were staring back at me.

The Re-Corrections:
A Remembered Memoir

Remembering is always the hardest part. Memory can be a touchy subject, even on the best of days. Conversations, encounters, passing glances that all seemed meaningful are now difficult to recall. While other moments, even more fleeting, moments that can not be measured in any known unit of time, surround me with a resounding clarity that seems as real today as it did in the distant (and even the not so distant) past.

Ok, I admit it. I keep digressing. It's hard to pay attention when you're surrounded by so much crap. Can I say crap? Will someone get offended by crap? Will the insinuation be too much? Or should I go with the more prosaic "stuff"? I don't know. Why make all of these decisions? Crap, stuff, junk, I mean the list could go on and on. Is this what you want to see me do? Can't you let me be in peace? I'm trying to create some context here for the narrative to follow. See, there I go again with the digressions. Where was I? Back to memory, yes my memories.

I would love to be able to tell you that I was born somewhere in the Carpathian Mountains, the third child of an illicit marriage between a Russian Orthodox priest and a Romanian nun who later gave me up for adoption to an English archaeologist who was working in central Romania. I would further love to tell you that an English archaeologist took me to London and after his untimely death on the steps of British Museum; I lived as a street urchin on the London Underground.

It was there, while riding the Northern line toward Tottenham Court Road one afternoon, a reporter from National Public Radio interviewed me for a piece he was recording about Bosnian orphans. I wasn't Bosnian but that didn't seem to matter at the time. My interview was subsequently broadcast to much critical acclaim. (The reporter eventually won the Pulitzer Prize for Best Reporting in the "Foreign Gritty Human Drama" category that year). It seemed that the Volvo driving, Starbucks drinking liberals who thrive on NPR really enjoyed the raw, earthy emotion in the story of a half Romanian street urchin who sold Orthodox Icons to London bankers in order to fund his Wellbutrin addiction.

After the broadcast, the reporter took my story (which I will later recount here) and wrote a best selling novel that made him extremely wealthy. Whether out of guilt or some fear that I would overcome my illiteracy, read the novel, and harbor some bitterness at being cheated from riches gained on the back of my suffering, he bribed two State Department officials and secured me a Visa to attend college in the United States.

Gaining admission to an unnamed Ivy League university solely on the basis of my short story about Albanian and Serbian shepherds engaged in a forbidden romance in 1960's era Yugoslavia, I was also awarded a MacArthur Foundation "genius" grant and given a half-million dollar advance to produce a screenplay on the subject of my story. "Moss Covered Valley", as it would be later called, was nominated for twelve academy awards as well the Palme de Orr at the Cannes Film Festival. But due to an overwhelming liberal bias in the judges, a film by Michael Moore entitled, "You Can call me Betty and I Can Call you Al Jazeera", won the award for Best Picture. I guess that being half Romanian wasn't un-American enough. I realized that if I was going to go anywhere in the world fifteen minute stardom I would have to convert to Islam. That was too radical, maybe. Prudent, could be. That, like the recriminations from a night of bingeing on Lipitor and Pinot Noir, would come later.

Never one to be deterred by a temporary setback, I published the screenplay as a short story in the New Yorker's annual fiction issue. John Updike called me the half-Romanian heir to his own legacy as the premier chronicler of post-modern middle class malaise in late 20th century America.

It was at this point, I began to develop occasional bouts of Amnesia. That means I would forget important things about my life on a regular basis. Have I told you this before? I can't remember.

Did I mention that the MacArthur Grant led to literary stardom and rock star like status that I had never imagined in the wildest of my Lexapro fueled binges. My celebrity only grew greater when people saw my photograph on the back flap of the hard back edition of my book "The Future is Forever". Sporting a Mohawk haircut, a red flannel shirt, wielding a rusty ax (to symbolize my chopping away at the literary traditions that preceded me), and standing beside a Paul Bunyan-esque team of blue oxen called the Pickles Patrol, I began to receive interview requests from television shows like "The View", "Late Night with David Letterman", as well as Anderson Cooper 360. I had truly reached the pinnacle of American literary stardom.

Somewhere between the television appearances and buying a home in the Hamptons, I found myself leading a group of Kurdish freedom fighters in southeastern Turkey. Again, I can't quite remember how I got there, but I know that I had did have amnesia, I remember having jetlag, and learning the Turkish words for, "no, I'm married" and "I'm trying to stop using heroin".

Did I mention I converted to Islam? I didn't change my name because I was able to convince the Kurds using remedial Kurdish that my given name, "Felipe Ramon Sanchez Windsor de Popotrescu" was indeed a genuine Islamic name in Romania. A risk, I know. I gambled that my comrades had never been to Romania and wouldn't know the difference. But then wouldn't it be my luck to meet the one Kurd working as a freedom fighter who had also done an MBA at the University of Bucharest. See, I've always been one to borrow trouble, is it any wonder I'm writing this as I'm confined to a rehab clinic for depressed people addicted to antidepressants? (I'll come back to that thought.)

It was after this elaborate ruse to show my radical Islamic street credibility to the Kurdish brethren when they revealed that they weren't Muslim after all. A few years back, they had met a group of traveling Nepalese gypsies who had also been devout Maoists. (Can someone be devout about a radical strain of militant atheism? Does devout have to relate to explicitly defined religious faith?) Digressions! See what I mean about the ADD, ADHD, Amnesia, and everything else with which I've been diagnosed?

After one evening with the Nepalese Maoists, the Kurds discarded their Korans for Mao's little red book and launched their very own proletariat revolution, Maoist style. (Albeit a Maoist style filtered and understood through both Nepalese and Kurdish thought. Remember, context is everything.)

The Kurds weren't the most active freedom fighters in southeastern Turkey. Between battles with the Turkish army and binges on opium bootlegged from ex-Taliban dealers in Afghanistan, they had managed to establish an underground newspaper to serve the entire Kurdish community. "The Cappadocian Chronicle" was a weekly broadsheet that carried everything from local soccer scores, results of the elementary school spelling bee, as well as the numbers of Turks killed by snipers over the previous seven day period. After copies of the New Yorker issue featuring "Moss Covered Valley" began to arrive in the guerilla camps, it was only a short time before the local tribal chiefs asked me to become the executive editor and publisher of the paper. Problems would soon arise. Because I didn't speak great Kurdish, I was unaware of many of the intricacies of Turkish law. I would later discover that printing anti-Turkish propaganda carried the death sentence in Turkey while attempting the murder of a Pope only warranted twenty years.

Though I didn't know it at the time, the Turks are very sensitive people. In fact, they'll probably be hurt terribly by merely reading of their perceived sensitivity. With that last sentence, I have risked my own death. If I'm ever caught trying to return to Turkey that last sentence will be entered into evidence against me and I'll be charged with, "Making Claims about Turks that could be perceived as Potentially Negative at Some Point in an Unknown Future." I know what you're thinking. Yes, it's punishable by death.

My tenure as editor in chief and publisher was an unqualified success. That was until I made the decision to reprint a series of controversial cartoons depicting the prophet Mohammed as an understudy for one of the lead roles in Broke Back Mountain. These cartoons had met much critical acclaim some months earlier when they were published throughout the three Baltic republics of Lithuania, Latvia, and Estonia. Though some Muslims had destroyed embassies in Liechtenstein and Monaco and new Fatwas were issued across the Muslim world, I thought that as former militant Muslims, my kooky band of crazy Kurdish commandos would love to poke fun at their former tradition. Remember, they're Maoists now. Or so I thought?

Apparently you can take a Kurd out of the Koran but you can't take the Muslim out of the Maoist. It was if they had never heard of Chairman Mao. Years of communist indoctrination out the window! Suddenly, as if by magic, they all wanted to be Muslim again but not just any old kind of Muslim. They wanted to be the highly offended, really angry Muslims-like you see on Fox News or PBS documentaries. Before I knew it, I was wearing an orange jumpsuit, kneeling before a cheap Kodak 8mm movie camera, while my former comrades donned ski masks and circled me with their automatic weapons.

Between takes of begging for my life in front of the camera and trying to figure a way out, I managed to convince a plurality of my captors that I had meant no harm by republishing the cartoons and had only wanted to provoke a debate about press freedom in our community. My goal had been to strengthen civic discourse in the public forum. In my reasoning, what harm had been done?

Having been given a third (or is it fourth) new lease on life, I wasn't quite ready to relinquish the inherent drama of the moment. Given the fact that I was surrounded by willing actors on the stage of life and was in possession of working movie camera, I began to see that I could make a low-budget independent short film about someone who is captured by insurgents in an unnamed Middle Eastern country and then after a prolonged captivity is able to convince the hostage takers that the hostage is in fact right and that they (the hostage takers) are wrong. In psychological circles, this is known as the Kurdish Condition (the polar opposite of the Stockholm Syndrome). After an impromptu session of brainstorming and scriptwriting on the back of an Istanbul phone book, we produced a film called "Talking Turkey".

I took my few possessions (satellite phone, a HP laptop, one maxed out American Express Card, keys to my ex-wife's Volvo, an Air France frequent flyer card, a charger for the sat phone, and one disposable BIC lighter) and the 8mm film reels, and began the long walk toward Park City, Utah and the Sundance Film Festival.

Richard Bryant

The Axis of Evil-Austrian Style

At first, I couldn't quite make out what they were chanting. But after a moment, I realized what I was hearing. The words were "Marg ba America" followed soon by "Marg ba Israel". Here's a travel tip, if you're in crowd of several hundred assorted angry Arabs, Iranians, and Austrian Trotskyite Socialists who start chanting Death to America and Death to Israel in Farsi, it's time to start heading for the exits. Or is it? Or should you pull out your digital camera, start taking pictures, and moving among the crowd? I could do both. I decided to stay.

Ok, back up a minute. You think I'm kidding, right? No, I'm not. Remember where I am. I'm not in Tehran. I'm not in Damascus. I'm not in Beirut. I'm in the center of historic Vienna, Austria.

Until this point, my day had been uneventful yet interesting. I had met with an Austrian bank official and then had late lunch. After lunch, I decided to go to Mozart's house and see where the great man lived. This year marks Mozart's 300th birthday and the Austrians have been celebrating all year. I left Mozart's house and began to wonder back toward the central square (St. Stephen's Platz). Instead of using the larger streets that I had taken earlier in the afternoon, I went through smaller, less traveled side streets.

Vienna's bewitching architecture makes it easy to forget you're not walking around the city in the summer of 1796. Externally, the city appears to have changed little in the intervening centuries. As I came to end of another narrow alley, I decided to turn right and move in the general direction of the square. By this time, I was really in the Viennese moment.

112

I was still humming Mozart. I half expected to meet Antonio Salieri as I turned the corner. But, instead of the masked Salieri, I ran into a sea of red flags and people gathering for what looked to be a large political demonstration. In an instant, I was jerked back into the political realities of 21st century.

The red flags were the first things that caught my eye. How can they not? They're red, after all. But these were not just any kind of red banners. They were Russian, or more correctly, Communist red. I know a thing or two about communist flags. After all, I do live in Moscow. I've seen my share. I even own an antique Soviet flag or two. Though on this sunny Friday afternoon, I found myself staring at red flags, the likes of which I hadn't seen since the May Day parade two months earlier. As I drew nearer to the crowd, I was able to pick out other flags. There were groups of Syrian flags, Lebanese flags, Palestinian flags, and even the flag of the Islamic Republic of Iran.

On one side of the square, a group of men were hastily erecting a stage and setting up microphones for speakers. I began to feel like Forrest Gump wandering around the Lincoln Memorial during that anti Vietnam War rally. If I wasn't careful, I'd be up on stage being asked my thoughts on the war in southern Lebanon. (And needless to say, I didn't expect a "Jenny" to come running out of the crowd yelling "Richard, Richard.")

It goes without saying that I stood out. At least I was certain that I did. Whether or not anyone else noticed was another matter. In my paranoid logic, it would take only one misplaced word or gesture to reveal my true identity. I didn't look Arab, that's a given. Even if had spent weeks growing a beard and dying what hair I have black, I still wouldn't

Richard Bryant

have looked like an Arab. With a bit of luck and only if I was pressed, could I possibly pass as a European (or Canadian).

I wanted to know if this demonstration was a planned gathering or a spontaneous expression of anti-Americanism. This is Europe and stranger things have happened. Structure, if it was going to be present, would provide a veneer of security if things got dicey. After idling around the Trotsky table for a few minutes I walked over to the main Palestinian table. To my surprise, it was a little light on the Jihadist propaganda but heavy on the Palestinian nationalism. Most of the material on offer was produced by one of the older groups that have dropped below the radar screens of many western observers of the Middle East. Today, the coverage is all about Hamas and Hezbollah. But thirty years ago, enemy number one was the Popular Front for the Liberation of Palestine (PFLP). The PFLP was a pseudo-Marxist group that once employed the infamous terrorist Carlos the Jackal. Mainly, they were secular nationalists instead of Islamic fascists. I knew they were still around but I didn't know to what extent. Like many others, I thought they had been eclipsed by the more militant and religiously inspired groups.

After what seemed like an eternity, an Arab woman emerged from the rear of the truck and began to organize and straighten the material sitting out on the table. "Ahh, she must work here," I said to myself. Again, not wanting to give myself away (or be beaten by an angry mob), I asked in my best broken English (with a heavy Slavic accent), "Speakers, are speakers going here to be?" She stopped (I thought to tell me how ridiculous I sounded) and without missing a beat she looked straight at me and said, "Yes".

114

"They will be starting in just a few minutes. You might want to stay near the front so you can hear them better."

"Thank you very much, I will do that." I hadn't been made.

"Do you hate America because they are free?"

"What?"

Let me back up a moment. I had lingered long enough to start to talk to people who were genuinely attending the demonstration. I was talking to an Iranian guy holding a Hezbollah flag. I had been standing next to him for a few minutes and had tried to strike up a casual conversation. What is a casual conversation for a death to America and Israel rally? The weather is always a good opener.

"Warm day for a demonstration, isn't it?" I asked. It was clear this agent of Islamic radicalism wasn't used to being asked about the weather by an American.

"Yeah, it's kind of hot. But not as hot as it is in Lebanon."

With that opening, I decided to pose my big question.

"Do you hate us because we're free?"

"What?"

"Do you hate America because they are free and because they espouse the liberal enlightenment values of freedom, liberal democracy, and human rights?"

Again, there were blank stares.

"That's what Americans have heard. You all hate us because we love freedom and you're opposed to freedom."

"No, we hate you because you're you," he stated emphatically.

"Because we're us," I asked.

"Yes, because you're America. It's got nothing to do with freedom. It's because you support Israel, you're not Muslim, and you're not us. Why do you ask?"

"Just curious," I said. I was thinking something completely different. I was thinking that the realities of the war on terror are being fought in the mountains of Afghanistan, the back alleys of Baghdad, and on the streets of Western Europe. If this is what the Muslims in Western Europe believe, how on Earth will we ever change the hearts and minds of those living in places like Basra or Kandahar?

To Beat the Devil

Some days I am convinced "we" didn't beat the Communism in the epic struggles of Cold War diplomacy. (By "we", I mean the good, God-fearing western capitalists as personified by the United States of America.) Read carefully what I said. I'm not saying that "they" won or that "we" lost. I am saying that the victory we collectively claimed as a culture wasn't the triumph as it is often portrayed.

The Cold War is still fought today. Only now, it is waged in different ways and in different places. Some scholars or politicians may talk about the legacy of the Cold War in the current geopolitical environment. Since 1991, the Cold War has evolved and adapted itself to the changing structures of politics and economics. It is not that the Cold War ended and we are merely picking up the pieces in Afghanistan, Chechnya, Bosnia, and elsewhere. No, the Cold War is being fought in each of those regions and in many others. It is only more diffused and less focused than in previous years. But without a doubt, it is the same war with the some key players. (This doesn't take into consideration the unfinished hostilities of the Korean War. The Korean War is the quintessential Cold War conflict, still unresolved after 56 years. Even today, the two countries which contribute the most to North Korea's meager existence are the People's Republic of China and the Russian Federation. That is no coincidence.) This is not a new idea. The Ancient Greeks understood conflict as a continuum of struggle that extended over many decades. You see this clearly in Thucydides' History of the Peloponnesian War.

What did we do? Did we know what we were doing? Did we defeat Communism? In a way, yes, we did. We defeated the official version of Communism as was practiced in the Soviet Union. Here's a comparison. Enron went out of business. But the ideologies of greed and deception that drove Enron out of business are still very much alive and well in other companies whose illegalities have yet to be discovered. Officially, the Soviet Union is out of business. Yet the ideology which drove the engine of state socialism is still breathing and living beneath the pock marked asphalt of the Moscow streets. Communism was deeply entrenched in every level of Soviet society that the simple act of lowering the Soviet flag on December 31st, 1991 was only a symbolic gesture. Yes, Eastern Europe was free. The occupying Soviet armies withdrew their tanks and returned to Mother Russia. But remember, there was no where for them to go from there. What do I mean? The Russians could pack up and leave East Germany, Hungary, and the Czech Republic. These countries were then free to develop along their own paths and grow into mature democracies. The Russians could not simply pack up and leave Russia. They were left with themselves, facing themselves, and unwilling to confront the reality of what they had wrought in the post-war world. We didn't defeat the Russians. We bankrupted an already bankrupt system and forced them to go back home, where they would be less obvious and less obstructive to the rest of the world.

It is nearly impossible to eradicate a deeply held belief when this is all a civilization has ever known. Communism was an ideology and worldview infecting each strata of Soviet society. Yet capitalism isn't the antibiotic it should be for the Russian people. (Capitalism is working on the macro level but at the micro-economic level it has yet to make a lasting impact.)

I see it at the grocery store and at the post office. I see it on the subway and the trolleybus. It is in these residual fortresses of socialist, mindless inefficiency that I wage a daily Cold War style struggle to maintain my own sanity. One question plaguing me from day to day is how do I take my own principled stand against these tenebrous forces without becoming an ugly American? The answer to that question depends on the given situation on the given day. Some days it is easier to deal with than others. However, on those days when I have a tiny victory over the remnants of the world that Lenin built and Stalin perfected, I can regain some strength and hope for the next battle that is as near as the next time I leave my front door.

I'm writing this not solely because Orwell caused me to reflect once more on the dystopian fantasy world in which I live. Orwell provides a way in which one may attempt understand the realities of the lingering, moribund socialist order. It is as if we are living in the yet unwritten sequel to 1984. Because to truly grasp what it takes to survive as a religious institution in post-Soviet Russia, it is necessary, indeed it is a requirement to understand what it means to live surrounded by fear, paranoia, mistrust, doubt, and suspicion. In short, you must enter the world of Winston Smith. That is incredibly hard for westerners to do. We so want to believe that a permanent moral shift occurred throughout the former USSR in the wake of Communism. Like the Apostle Paul's instantaneous redemption on the Damascus road, we have wanted to believe that all of Russia saw a blinding light, admitted the errors of the past, and came to know Christ in the blink of an eye.

Clearly, the current situation is a far cry from the late Soviet repression of the Brezhnev era. However, the questions raised by dissidents such as Sakharov and Solzhenitsyn are still reasonable, needed, and valid questions today. Those five hallmarks totalitarian rule (fear, paranoia, mistrust, doubt, and suspicion) are tools which are readily and regularly used to enforce the will of those who hold the power. This is not something that should be taken lightly by anyone observing Russia from beyond her borders.

The old ways have not completely died. In the past fifteen years, Russia has stumbled through a deepening stupor to regain a renewed sense of national identity under the leadership of President Putin. It is neither accident nor coincidence that as a former KGB officer he has surrounded himself with those whom he shares a common professional past. They form an alumni association like no other in modern history. These men are sometimes credited with reshaping Russia into a modern nation. Momentarily placing our notions of modernity aside, that which western observers call reshaping is in reality a reinforcing of the age old traditions of Slavic autocracy.

Many still share the belief that anything in the west's interest cannot be in Russia's interest. If there are values that are crucial to western democratic society then they must be mistrusted and regarded as suspect in the hybrid east-west Russian culture. Russia's place in the world is defined by the polarities separating Russia's priorities from other countries. It is in this environment that public policies are made and implemented. Many of these policies are fundamentally at odds with the values and principles inherent in any democratic society. The freedom of religious choice is critical to creating a functioning civil democratic society. If we truly care about promoting religious diversity, we must also care about the state of religious freedom in Russia. If we only care about spreading the gospel (doing our thing, our way, oblivious to the world around us), it is as if we are living in a vacuum that ignores the political and social realities of modern Russia. We will be doing only half the job and when things begin to go south, we will have only ourselves to blame.

Can you ever know a place? I know people (non Russians) who have lived in this country for years, speak fluent Russian, studied every imaginable aspect of Russian history, and built sound relationships with both rich and poor who readily admit that Russia remains an eternal enigma. On the other hand, I've known some people that after three or four 10 day mission trips cannot be told anything about Russia, they know it all. It is truly amazing how easy it is to develop a nuanced and comprehensive picture of life in modern Russia when you see it once a year during the summer.

My sarcasm may be strong but to renew our commitment to serious preparation before we undertake our mission enterprise we must realize that we can do more to be informed and invested in the lives of those whom we assist. The vulnerability of readily admitting that we do not know it all is the first step to learning what we can do. In short, there are degrees of not knowing.

Investment remains the key. Investment is much more than a monetary commitment. We must invest the totality of our commitment to the work occurring in Russia. Money alone will not lay the foundation for the future of the church in Russia. There are some people who have realized what must be done to ensure our continued growth Russia. We need more of them.

The Real Russia

Some visitors to Russia say to truly know Russia, one must leave Moscow. Rubbish, I say! Rubbish! Moscow is as much part of Russia as any other region. I would argue that to truly appreciate what is happening in Russia-the political, social, and economic changes wrought by the collapse of Communism-you can see without ever leaving Moscow.

I'm sure people make this same argument about the United States. Many Americans would say that New York City isn't representative of the United States as a whole. How could a melting pot of beliefs, cultures, languages, and ideas be anything but representative of the United States? Large cities are part of the rich cultural fabric that creates the entirety of a people.

Yet, despite the obvious, I still hear insistences that the real Russia is only to be found beyond the borders of Moscow. The problem is that when some visitors refer to leaving Moscow, they believe that they are embarking on time traveling journey to an idyllic, bucolic Chekhovian village. It reminds of a time in Armenia just a few years ago. Someone once told me that if you wanted to see the real Armenia, you had to go to the villages. This presumes that villages have some type of authenticity that cities inherently lack. For most outside observers of the former USSR, the idea of the "village" still personifies the quintessence of the Russian soul.

Maybe that's right. I say this because Moscow is a village, albeit a large village of 14 million people. It is the giant excrescence of a market town, lacking the elegance of St. Petersburg but offering a far deeper look into what drives modern Russia. The key is learning how to understand what you're seeing.

Russians are hard to read. Mannerism, body language, and spoken language all contribute to understanding the subtleties of human interaction. Many of these cultural variables that are central to life in Russia depend on practices that can only be learned by years of experience.

Here's an example. I have yet to uncover the fascination behind watching televised poker games. It is not that I am unable to understand the game, the rules, or the strategy behind the moves. I do. It is that the pleasure of watching others play cards is lost on me. The mystery of televised poker grows ever deeper when you realize you're watching people attempting to mask their emotions and expressions in order to with the game. If you're watching people hide behind masks (sunglasses or hats), what are you really watching? Is it their hands laying the cards on the table? I don't know. I make this point for one reason. Moving across Moscow is like watching 14 million poker players passing each other the sidewalks, buses, and metros.

The country that gave birth to Anton Chekhov has birthed generations of actors. When free expression was more severely controlled, the Russians learned that a single word, a misplaced expression, or an ill-timed smile could have life altering consequences. Thus, the mask of emotional control was deeply ingrained at all levels of society.

Wearing the mask is now a habit. Like the ubiquitous smoking and 9am drinking, it is seemingly inseparable and unavoidable in modern Russia. Occasionally, cracks in the masks may begin to appear. Maybe it is fatigue or a simple admission that they are in a role they are no longer willing to play.

Talk to the Hand

What's in a hand? If the five thousand people I saw gathered this afternoon around Christ the Savior Cathedral were to be asked, they would say a great deal. They came to see a hand. Not just any hand, but THE hand. It was the hand of the man who laid his hands on the head of the Son of God-who was also his cousin. Confused? Let me explain.

In the year 30 AD, or so the story goes, the son of a Galilean carpenter made his way south from the shores of the Sea of Galilee to the banks of the Jordan River. There, the carpenter's son's cousin was living a rough existence as an itinerant preacher and teacher. The Jordan Rived based cousin had begun a practice of ritual purification that came be known as baptism. Many of the people who came to hear the cousin speak also wanted to be baptized. They would wade into the water and at the appropriate moment, the cousin would pour water (or submerge-the evidence is not conclusive) over the head of the individual. This water was a symbolic cleansing of sins and past iniquities.

The other cousin, the one from Galilee, came to see his relative and be baptized. The Galilean carpenter's son was duly baptized and the rest, as they say, is history. I was talking about the hand. This isn't a Bible study lesson. I need to get back to the hand. The hand, on display at the Christ the Savior Cathedral in Moscow this week, is said to be the hand of John the Baptizer.

I've seen a few relics in my travels. Jerusalem is chocked full of them. Many churches in England and elsewhere in Europe have competing relics. In the middle ages, the crusaders ransacking Jerusalem regularly brought back the same relics from the same saint. The relative status and importance of a church was determined the quality of their relics. In both western and eastern Christianity, you were nobody unless you had the best bones.

It's not unusual to find a cathedral in England and an abbey in Austria both claiming to posses the same body part from the same saint. Most of the relics that I've seen would be "B" grade or "C" grade relics at best. These relics are from minor saints and martyrs who don't figure prominently in the grand scheme of Christian history. I had normally thought of relics as a Roman Catholic or western phenomenon. That is because there is really little written in English about Eastern Orthodoxy and relics. As I learned to today, simply because I hadn't heard about any or read about any in English, doesn't mean that a reliquary tradition exists in Orthodoxy. It does, in big way.

I read about the "hand" in the paper. On the cover of today's issue of the Moscow Times was a photograph of a woman holding her young child up to kiss a box that was said to contain the hand (right or left, I don't know) of John the Baptist. Admittedly, it's not everyday you see a hand on the front page of the paper, especially in Moscow. Being the religious type that I am, I was intrigued by the photograph. If John the Baptizer's hand is in town, I ought to go and see it. After all, how many times do you get the opportunity to see the hand of the man who baptized Jesus?

I guessed the hand wasn't here on a one night tour so I decided to head that way after finishing some errands in town. Stepping off the subway station closest to the cathedral hosting John's hand, I noticed that there was fair number of folks coming back on to the metro as if they had just seen the "hand". How did I know that they had seen the hand? Some were wearing t-shirts that read, "I've just seen the hand of John the Baptist". No, just kidding. It was a greater number than usually used this station on a weekday afternoon. Outside, I saw a crowd but nothing that struck me as out of the ordinary. Then I noticed the metal detectors, the police, the line coming from the front door, and the five thousand people stretching for three city blocks. From the sheer numbers of people and the police presence one would have thought a rock star or head of state was inside the building having negations about Iran and nuclear weapons. (Bono meets Putin in the cause of world peace?) I had never witnessed such a display for such a small relic. There is really not much security at the Holy Sepulcher in Jerusalem or the Church of the Nativity in Bethlehem. But this isn't Israel, now is it?

Apparently it is on loan from somewhere in Montenegro. I guess it's ultimately on loan from John the Baptist's arm but he's not been available for comment. I hope it will be here for several days. Maybe I'll get back down there after the big rush. I don't want to miss my big chance to talk to the hand.

Anna Politkovskaya: Martyr for the Truth

"Utrum veritas sit fortior inter vinum et regem et mulierem."
St. Thomas Aquinas

In the Quaestio quodlibetalis XII, 14, Saint Thomas Aquinas asks this question: Which is more powerful in a given society, is it the power of the king, the influence of wine, the charms of a woman, or the strength of truth? It is a series of questions for the ages. The Angelic Doctor didn't realize it but from his perch in 13th century Italy he was also describing 21st century Russia. (Perhaps this also helps us to realize the essential medieval character of contemporary Russian society.)

Where is the power concentrated in 21st century Russia? From my perspective, it is centered somewhat in three of those disparate locales. It is in the power of the king, whose name is Vladimir. It is in the influence of wine that flows everywhere. It can be found in the alluring charms of the Slavic women. Though the strength of the truth is something that that is fighting and dying to remain alive. The force of truth, the standard by which virtue is measured, Aquinas writes, will only come at the price of blood and tears. He was right.

"I must be crazy," I muttered as I opened my eyes. The room was still pitch black and I could hear that it was raining hard and coming down fast outside. Although my alarm clock claimed the time was 6:37 AM, the exterior darkness and rain told my brain that it had to be much earlier. Getting used to the sun coming up later at these northern latitudes is something that takes an adjustment. Thus, going to church was the last thing on my mind. I had stayed up too late watching television coverage of the murder of a prominent Russian journalist.

After about five more minutes, I managed convince my brain that my eyes were correct and started to move. It has been difficult for me to come to terms with the fact that it takes forty-five minutes to an hour to get to church with much of that time on foot. It's a long walk on a beautiful day. On a day like today, it's going to be a long, hard slog. As I was walking up the hill on Tverskaya Avenue, feeling the water squish in my shoe, I was wondering what it would be like if most Americans had to walk to church. I guessed that many of our churches would be empty. By the time I arrived, I was five minutes late and soaking wet. Thankfully, I found a towel and made my way to the sanctuary.

As the few who gathered for the early service mingled in the narthex after the service for coffee, the conversation turned in one inevitable direction. Everyone was talking about the murder of the journalist Anna Politkovskaya. It is hard to overemphasize the effect that the killing of this one woman is having on Russia today. She was, without exception, the most famous journalist in Russia. She had survived war in Chechnya, being poisoned, and had to flee Russia because of death threats. Her life ended late Saturday afternoon in the elevator of her downtown Moscow apartment building. The killer's calling card, an untraceable Stechkin pistol left at the scene with four spent shell casings, bore the familiar hallmarks of a contract assassination. This may seem odd to those of you reading in this in the United States. After all, you might be saying, journalists die in America. Yes, they die covering wars in Iraq and Afghanistan. They are not gunned down in the homes and apartment buildings in broad daylight. Twelve journalists have been assassinated in Russia in the past six years alone. Since 1999, over fifty journalists have been murdered.

Let me try and put this into context. Imagine a well respected journalist (male or female) known for hard hitting, yet honest reporting that is critical of the government, the defense establishment, and economic corruption. Bob Woodward comes to mind. Someone like him, that's the type of person I'm talking about. Now imagine that this person is gunned down on the steps of their suburban home. What would that do to America? When journalists are killed and wounded in Iraq, that's a big enough story. What would this be like? Would the media critics claim, as they do when a journalist is killed in Iraq, "American soldiers are killed everyday and they don't make as big a fuss about them and here one journalist gets injured and you'd think it's the end of the world."

If I've heard that statement (or similar) once, I've heard it a hundred times. This is part of the reason Anna Politkovskaya's death will not faze people in America. Because both sides of the political spectrum in the US believe the media is biased in one direction or another, we have trouble imagining a place where investigative journalism; journalism which is openly critical and hostile to the government in power is the only way to get the truth. In Russia, honest journalists have an obligation to be biased against the government. If they're not, they are simply mouthpieces for the government or corporate interests. It makes me think that maybe we should start rethinking our own definition of bias.

Russia is a country where people who question the system and expose the truth are regularly killed. It is a sad, tragic, and frustrating fact of life. Russia isn't unique in this respect. Other countries are as brutal if not more so. But think for a moment what it is like for the people who live here everyday with that fear. Pull yourself out of your comfort zone and put yourself into their uncomfortable Russian shoes. Hard, isn't it?

According to street parlance, it is the Russian verb zakazat', which means "to order", that you would use if you wanted to have someone killed. That's the same verb I use when I order a pizza or purchase a plane ticket. However, if it is spoken to the right people and you say you want to "order someone", then it means you want them killed by a contract killer. It is that easy. A few years ago, the Moscow Times published an article on contract killing in Russia. Using informants and other sources of information, they were able to piece together a price list for contract killing in Russia. Considering inflation has probably affected these prices as well, here's what they found. For about 150,000 dollars, it was possible to have a prominent member of the government murdered. For between 50-75 thousand dollars, depending on the journalist, they too could be eliminated. For as little as 150 dollars, your noisy neighbor who plays his stereo too loud at four o'clock in the morning could be executed. They knew this because it has happened. This wasn't some black Russian humor that made its way into print.

It doesn't take much to realize human life has little value for many Russians. Whether it is the rampant alcoholism or smoking, life isn't seen by many people as something worth a great deal of effort. In a great irony, the greatest value that many lives have is the value ascribed to them by those who specialize in taking life. In this warped economy of human life, the United Methodist Church finds itself attempting to present a viable religious alternative to the dominant culture of violence and nihilism. On days like today, I cannot help but feel that we are woefully unprepared.

This makes me think about one of the central themes of the New Testament. Jesus Christ said that he came to, "bring life and bring it more abundantly." Tell me this: How do you preach about an abundant life in a place where it can be taken for pocket change? How does the church in Russia (and Eurasia) talk about abundant life in such a way that it doesn't sound trite, banal, or written for middle class American Methodists?

Sure, you can step out in front of a bus, be hit by a drunk driver, or fall victim to any number of freak accidents and die. Those random occurrences know no geographic boundaries. This is different. Moscow is a city that functions, thrives, and moves at a breakneck pace. Yet, beneath the surface, obscured by the frenetic movement is a corrosive culture of fear and evil.

This reminds me, once again, that the world is not as black and white as we would like it to be. The nice divisions of light and dark, order and disorder, right and wrong are not as hard and fast as we want to believe. In order to understand the chaos that surrounds us, we need those clear demarcations. Yet in Russia, amidst the chaos, there are no clear demarcations, save one–it was lying in the elevator of a Moscow apartment building on Saturday afternoon. The strength of the truth was there gasping for air, waiting to be revived just beyond the body of Anna Politkovskaya.

Epilogue

Leaving on the Midnight Plane to Georgia

Friday into Saturday, 12:30 AM, the departure lounge, Vienna International Airport, the Republic of Austria.

The newspapers tell me Kurt Waldheim is dead. Austria is in mourning. It is difficult to be sympathetic for a Waffen SS intelligence officer who helped supervise the deportation of thousands of Jews from the Balkans and then lied about it. The Austrians do not seem to mind. In truth, I am feigning my indignation. At this hour, it is too hard to care about much of anything. I am in Vienna waiting on a midnight plane to Georgia. I am going back to the Caucasus to find a simpler place and time. It is a world I left behind not so long ago. Though tonight, I am going alone. No one is going to be right by my side. However, I am still planning on taking that ride.

Perhaps, because I am into my fifth cup of high-grade Austrian espresso; I am jittery, nervous, and exhausted. I recognize this feeling: four days of little sleep, too much caffeine, not enough Wellbutrin, and burned out adrenalin supplies-a giddy, fluttering kind of high which tells me the crash is coming. That same feeling you get when you've been told, "it's not going to work" or "I need a real relationship" in an early morning long distance phone call. The feeling you get when you realize nobody you know now or used to know then gives a damn about you tonight. The crash is coming.

But when will it come? When I am somewhere over the Black Sea at 25,000 feet? The likelihood of a panic attack, forcing a landing in Sofia and spending the next three days undergoing psychiatric evaluations in a

Bulgarian mental hospital, seems a real possibility. How will I explain that? How much longer? Will it be now or ten minutes from now? Will Bob's Big Hillbilly Blue Grass band carry me on board the Airbus A-300? The tension is part of the exhaustion. It is almost too much to bear. The stress is all that remains of my last adrenalin rush. The possibility of complete mental and physical collapse is very real now...

...but collapse is out of the question: as a solution or a bargain basement alternative to reality, it is unacceptable. Indeed. This is the moment of truth; I am preparing to cross the fine line between control and disaster. There is a point when you're no longer exhausted. A point when the fateful line between fatigue and collapse dissolves into oblivion. That's where I am, in Vienna, Austria.

I was in Moscow. One hour on the runway in Moscow. Traffic jams on the road. Traffic jams in the sky. Moscow is a town founded on the concepts of flight and delay. People are always fleeing Moscow for somewhere else. When so many people are trying to move, delays are inevitable. What can I say; Moscow is a place many people can't wait to leave. I didn't intend to take the midnight plane to Georgia. The ticket provided by Austrian Airlines claimed our departure would occur around 10:30. They lied.

What do I do? What can I do? I sit there and take it. I listen to the silence of delay. I begin to come to grips with the lack of meaningful communication from anyone. So do the others. They begin to make the same adjustments. There are the Georgians waiting to go home. There is Bob's Big Hillbilly Blue Grass Band, on their way to spread international friendship with indigenous American folk music. I guess they are kind of like me, people trying to do what they know how to do best for other people. And as tired as I am, that one small fact still gives me a small bit of hope.

The Moscow Diaries

Richard Bryant

The Moscow Diaries

Richard Bryant

The Moscow Diaries

Richard Bryant

The Moscow Diaries

Richard Bryant

Index

About the Author

Richard Bryant is known for overcoming extraordinary obstacles in search of the truth. Whether searching for Plato's cave or confronting the realities of post-Soviet bureaucracy, Richard has made a career of bypassing professional academics, bribing border guards, avoiding military checkpoints, and ignoring conventional wisdom to bring his unique perspective to bear on complex religious, social, and political questions.

In his travels through some of the world's most menacing and inhospitable places, Richard has shared risks with his hosts and often has become an accidental witness to history-shaping events. Over the past decade, he has lived among Muslim villagers in West Africa, witnessed the bizarre voodoo rituals of Togolese voodoo priests, been blessed by the Dalai Lama, journeyed through civil war ravaged Liberia and Sierra Leone, wandered Yugoslavia's hinterlands in the era before the Dayton Peace Accord, and walked through the no man's land between Armenia and Azerbaijan.

In addition to Russian, Richard speaks colloquial Ukrainian, idiomatic Armenian, and very basic Mandarin Chinese.

Richard holds degrees from the University of North Carolina at Greensboro and Duke University. He has studied Russian and East European Studies at universities in the United Kingdom and in the former Soviet Union.

www.ingramcontent.com/pod-product-compliance
Lightning Source LLC
Chambersburg PA
CBHW021153020426
42331CB00003B/44